THE EGYPTIAN MUMMY
SECRETS AND SCIENCE

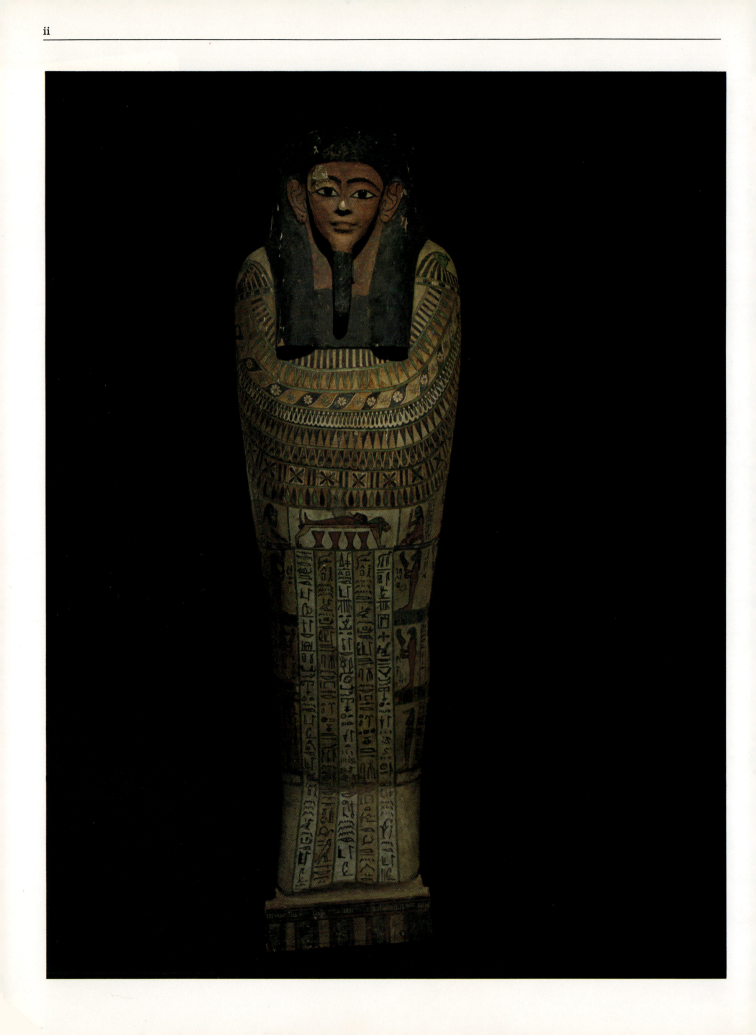

UNIVERSITY MUSEUM HANDBOOK 1

THE EGYPTIAN MUMMY
SECRETS AND SCIENCE

MASCA
Stuart Fleming
Bernard Fishman

EGYPTIAN SECTION
David O'Connor
David Silverman

COFFIN LID FOR THE MUMMY OF DJED-HAPI
Wood
L., 1.83 m.
Provenance unknown
Third Intermediate Period, *circa* 750 B.C.

(See also **96-98**)

Published by
THE UNIVERSITY MUSEUM
University of Pennsylvania
Philadelphia
1980

Library of Congress Cataloging in Publication Data
Main entry under title:

The Egyptian mummy.

  (University Museum handbooks)
  Bibliography: p.
  1. Mummies—Egypt. 2. Funeral rites and
ceremonies—Egypt. 3. Diseases—Egypt. I. Fleming,
Stuart James. II. Series: Pennsylvania. University
Museum. University Museum handbooks.
DT62.M7E35   393′.3′0932   80-20555
ISBN 0-934718-38-5

PREFACE

This book is an introduction to the history of mummification in Egypt. Essentially mummification was a religious practice, but it was also an unusual example of early science, for the embalmers experimented over time with a variety of techniques intended to preserve human bodies in as life-like a form as possible. The development of mummification, however, can be properly understood only in the context of the complex ideas the Egyptians had about life after death, so the essentials of these are also described and analyzed in the following pages. Our knowledge of these ideas is greatly helped by the extraordinary funerary art and archaeology of the Egyptians, in which they depicted in vivid detail their concepts of the nature of the funerary gods and of deceased humans and the character of the afterlife itself. Scenes from the walls of tomb chapels, funerary statues, decorated coffins and papyri and many other artifacts are used in this book to illustrate the variety and inventiveness of Egyptian funerary beliefs.

Equally important, the book describes the ways in which our knowledge of ancient Egyptian health and disease patterns has been very much enlarged by the scientific study of Egyptian mummies. Through their art, and through archaeological remains, we can reconstruct the environment and the way of life of the Egyptians in a detailed way possible for few other ancient cultures. Autopsy and x-radiography of mummies reveal, sometimes in extraordinary detail, the physical effects of environment and custom upon the Egyptians; the remains of parasites, the traces of infectious diseases, the result of injuries incurred by accident or from malice, the effects of diet upon dentition are only some of the topics covered in the relevant sections of this book.

The Egyptian Mummy: Secrets and Science was written in conjunction with an exhibit of the same name, on show at the University Museum of the University of Pennsylvania from September, 1980 to August, 1981; the exhibit itself, the first major review of Egyptian mummification and the scientific study of mummies to be mounted in the United States, was partially funded by a grant of $137,064 by the National Endowment for the Humanities to MASCA and the Egyptian Section of the Museum. However, while the book is illustrated by many artifacts from the exhibit and covers (in much greater detail) the same general themes, it is an independent treatment of Egyptian mummification, funerary beliefs and the scientific study of mummies, and not a catalogue or a handbook to the exhibit.

The following acknowledgments are appropriate: to the various scientists, including Prof. W. Miller, Dr. C. White, Dr. D. Muncey, and Dr. B. Doughty (of the University of Pennsylvania), and Prof. J. E. Harris (of the University of Michigan) for their advice so willingly given; to Helen Schenck (MASCA) for her thorough attention to the documentation of artifacts illustrated in the book; to Susan d'Auria and Alan Morrow (Egyptian Section) for their research on several of the captions to the plates; to William Clough and Harmer Frederick Schoch of the University Museum's Photographic Section for their patience and efficiency in provision of the bulk of the book's artwork; to Nicholas Hartmann of MASCA, Dr. J. Ruffle of the University of Durham, Dr. W. V. Davies of the British Museum, Dr. R. David of the Manchester Museum, Dr. C. Lilyquist and Mary Doherty at the Metropolitan Museum of Art, New York, for exceptional help with other essential illustrations; to Geraldine Bruckner for her skilful editing, and to Martha Phillips for her thoughtful design of the artwork; to Virginia Greene for her supervision of the conservation of the artifacts before their photography; and indeed to everyone who has contributed in the production of a book which we hope will prove enjoyable to read for both the academic community and the public at large.

Stuart Fleming   David O'Connor
Bernard Fishman   David Silverman
MASCA   EGYPTIAN SECTION

CHRONOLOGY OF ANCIENT EGYPT

Predynastic Period (Upper Egypt)

Badarian	ca. 4800-4200 B.C.
Nagada I	ca. 4200-3700 B.C.
Nagada II	ca. 3700-3250 B.C.
Nagada III	ca. 3250-3100 B.C.

Archaic Period

Dynasty I	ca. 3100-2900 B.C.
Dynasty II	ca. 2900-2750 B.C.

Old Kingdom

Dynasty III	ca. 2750-2680 B.C.
Dynasty IV	2680-2544 B.C.
Dynasty V	2544-2407 B.C.
Dynasty VI	2407-ca. 2260 B.C.

First Intermediate Period

Dynasties VII, VIII, IX	ca. 2260-2175 B.C.
Dynasty X	ca. 2175-2035 B.C.
Dynasty XI (first part)	2134-2061 B.C.

Middle Kingdom

Dynasty XI (second part)	2061-1991 B.C.
Dynasty XII	1991-1784 B.C.

Second Intermediate Period

Dynasty XIII	1784-1668 B.C.
Dynasty XIV	1720-1665 B.C.
Dynasty XV (Hyksos)	1668-1560 B.C.
Dynasty XVI (Hyksos)	1665-1565 B.C.
Dynasty XVII	1668-1570 B.C.

New Kingdom

Dynasty XVIII	1570-1293 B.C.
Dynasty XIX	1293-1185 B.C.
Dynasty XX	1185-1070 B.C.

Third Intermediate Period

Dynasty XXI	1070-946 B.C.
Dynasty XXII	946-712 B.C.
Dynasty XXIII	828-ca. 665
Dynasty XXIV	718-685 B.C.
Dynasty XXV (Nubian)	767-656 B.C.

Saite Period

Dynasty XXVI	685-525 B.C.

Late Period

Dynasty XXVII (Persian)	525-404 B.C.
Dynasty XXVIII	404-399 B.C.
Dynasty XXIX	399-380 B.C.
Dynasty XXX	380-343 B.C.

Persian Reconquest	343-332 B.C.
Ptolemaic Period	332-31 B.C.
Roman Period	31 B.C.-A.D. 395
Byzantine Period	A.D. 395-641
Arab Conquest	begins A.D. 641

We are indebted to Professor Klaus Baer (Oriental Institute, Chicago) for his permission to use this unpublished chronology based upon his most recent research.

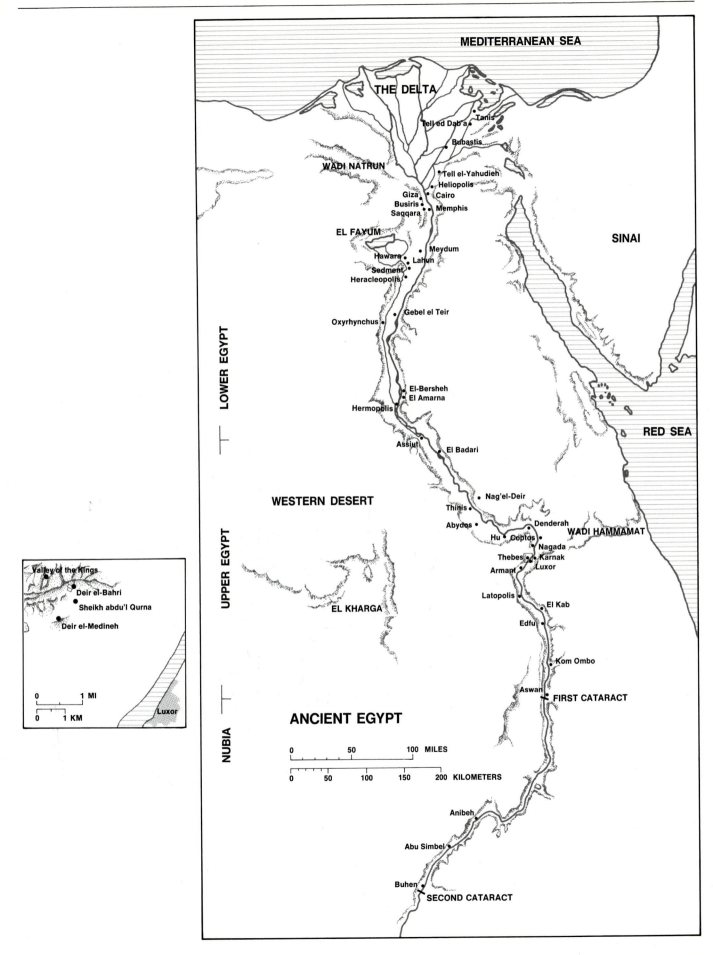

MEDITERRANEAN SEA

THE DELTA

Tanis
Tell ed Dab'a
Bubastis

WADI NATRUN

Tell el-Yahudieh
Heliopolis
Giza   Cairo
Busiris
Saqqara   Memphis

EL FAYUM

SINAI

Meydum
Hawara   Lahun
Sedment
Heracleopolis

Gebel el Teir

Oxyrhynchus

LOWER EGYPT

El-Bersheh
El Amarna
Hermopolis

RED SEA

Assiut   El Badari

WESTERN DESERT

Nag'el-Deir
Thinis

Abydos   Denderah
Hu   Coptos   WADI HAMMAMAT
Nagada
Thebes   Karnak
Armant   Luxor

UPPER EGYPT

Latopolis   El Kab

EL KHARGA

Edfu

Kom Ombo

Aswan   FIRST CATARACT

ANCIENT EGYPT

0   50   100 MILES

0   50   100   150   200 KILOMETERS

NUBIA

Anibeh

Abu Simbel

Buhen   SECOND CATARACT

Valley of the Kings
Deir el-Bahri
Sheikh abdu'l Qurna
Deir el-Medineh

0   1 MI
0   1 KM
Luxor

GLOSSARY

Canopic (jar)
The jars used to store the mummified internal organs extracted by the embalmers gained this label because of a mistaken link made early in Egyptological research. Canopus, the helmsman of Menelaus, figured in a Greek legend and was buried at a town of the same name in the Nile Delta. There, Canopus was actually worshipped in the form of a jar.

Cartonnage
A thin sheet of material prepared from linen strips stiffened by the addition of glue and plaster. From the Late period onwards, fragments of papyrus documents were a common substitute for the linen.

Cartouche
An elongated oval outline within which, from the Fourth Dynasty on, pharaoh's names were written. Its form seems to have its origins in a sign representing a knot of rope, looped so that it is never ending.

Cataract
A stretch of rapids interrupting the flow of the Nile and caused by the presence of granite outcrops in the otherwise sandstone geology of Nubia. There are six major cataracts between Aswan and Khartoum: all were hazards to navigation. Indeed, the Second Cataract was impassable except during the annual inundation.

Encaustic
A method of painting popular in the Graeco-Roman period of Egyptian history. It involved application of the pigments in a vehicle of beeswax, the paint layer then being fixed by heat.

Faience
A general term used for the turquoise-blue alkaline glazed objects, the production of which was well established by the Archaic Period. The body of the ware is principally powdered quartz, with some additive such as natron or soda-lime to provide a binding medium.

Hieratic (script)
The normal form of script used throughout Egyptian history, it derived from the hieroglyphs of monumental sculpture, but is distinguished from them by a general lack of pictorial character. It evolved into demotic script in the seventh century B.C. in northern Egypt and thus became the everyday script of the Late, Ptolemaic and Roman periods.

Mastaba
From the Arabic word for bench, it is now used to describe the free-standing tombs of the early dynastic era. The basic form of the superstructure of a mastaba is a rectangle with a flat roof and vertical mud-brick or slightly-inclined stone walls.

Mummy
The word mummy probably came from the Persian word mummia meaning bitumen, following a mistaken idea that the bodies preserved in ancient Egypt were black because they had been soaked in bitument.

Ostracon
Flake of limestone or a potsherd used as a cheap substitute for papyrus, particularly during the Nineteenth and Twentieth Dynasties.

Papyrus
The main Egyptian writing material, and an important export. Sheets were made by cutting the pith of the plant into strips laid horizontally and vertically. Beating the strips together made the plant's natural starch form an adhesive. Separate sheets were gummed together to form rolls.

Shawabti
From the end of the Middle Kingdom this small statuette was an important part of the funerary equipment. In the Eighteenth Dynasty shawabtis began to combine, somewhat incongruously, a likeness of the mummified body of the deceased with various agricultural tools held in the statuette's tightly crossed hands. This was a reflection of the two concepts the ancient Egyptians attached to shawabtis: a substitute for the body, and a worker who could act as the deceased's deputy when he was called upon to perform various manual tasks in the afterlife.

Stela
In a funerary context, a slab of stone bearing texts and reliefs which integrated with the overall decoration of the tomb. (Later stelae were often made of wood; then the reliefs were replaced by paintings.)

Vignette
In Egyptian literature, a simple illustration which tried to capture the essence of the textual material close to it in papyri such as the "Book of the Dead."

Vizier
The highest official of the administration, whose post was already a recognized one in the Archaic Period. In the New Kingdom, there were two viziers, one at Memphis, the other at Thebes, each wielding appreciable power; but after this time the importance of this post appears to have declined steadily.

CONTENTS

——————

COLOR PLATES

I. THE SETTING

EARLY SETTLEMENTS

Today the Nile river has been subdued by the great Aswan dam, located some 650 miles south of Cairo. With the river's flow now regularized and predictable, the farmer can be assured of enough water throughout the year to produce several harvests. But it was not always this way.

In ancient times Egyptian life was dominated by the rhythm of the Nile. From June through September rains in the highlands of Ethiopia would swell the Blue Nile, so that after its turbulent waters joined the sluggish White Nile, at Khartoum, the river would burst its banks along the length of the Nile Valley. Rich silt caught up in the rush of waters would settle upon the land, to nurture the next harvest once the flood had receded.

PREDYNASTIC BURIAL
L., 0.95 m.

Reconstructed using artifacts of the Nagada II phase of predynastic Egypt, *circa* 3500 B.C.

During the fourth millennium B.C., Egyptians were buried in shallow, sand-filled graves. Heated directly by the sun, the sand helped the bodies to dessicate naturally before decay destroyed their human appearance. (This fact may have suggested to the Egyptians that such preservation was necessary for a happy afterlife.) Later, after 3000 B.C., when graves were deeper, artificial means of preserving the body from decay had to be found; and so the techniques of mummification were developed.

Predynastic burials were usually contracted in position, apparently imitating a state of sleep. (This positioning may reflect a desire to save labor when the grave was being dug.) From the earliest times the dead were supplied with items needed to continue their normal life in the afterlife. Such items might include pottery vessels for food and drink, a slate palette upon which pigment for green eye-paint powder was ground, an ivory hairpin, and an elaborately shaped flint knife.

(University Museum: Lower Egyptian Gallery)

About seven thousand years ago, settlements sprung up some thirty miles south of the city of Assiut. Their inhabitants, called Badarians today after the modern village of El Badari where they were first found, looked towards the Nile for the source of their prosperity. In years of ample inundation, the villagers, themselves well-fed, could use the surplus of their crops as barter for luxury goods including copper from the Sinai (far to the northeast) and decorative shells from the Red Sea. Their goats and sheep were well-fattened, so that there was an adequate supply of meat and milk.

But the Nile was unpredictable. Excessive flood could sweep away entire villages and decimate livestock: too little flood would leave large expanses of farmland unirrigated, bringing the threat of famine. The Badarians could not conceive of human life as patterned differently from the natural cycles of growth, death and rebirth. Badarian burial customs indicate for the first time a belief in an afterlife similar to life in the Nile Valley and requiring the same simple material goods. Their shallow graves contained finely polished pottery vessels as well as coarse wares for domestic use; bone fish-hooks and flint blades adapted for either hunting or for dressing skins; modest personal possessions such as garments of cloth or skin, and ornamental strings of blue-glazed beads, bone bracelets and ivory hair combs.

The disposition and nature of these grave goods show us the funeral ritual of Egypt in its embryonic stage. The body itself is carefully covered with reed matting or an animal skin and sometimes decorated with a paste comprising the green mineral, malachite, ground up and mixed with castor oil. The smooth slate palette used to grind this malachite was usually placed close to the face of the deceased.

Amulets in the shape of hippopotamus and gazelle adorned the body.

Occasionally the bodies of small animals, such as dogs and sheep, were wrapped in linen and buried in the same cemeteries with the same care accorded the Badarians themselves. This action implies that these creatures too would have an afterlife, but little light can be shed on this custom since it does not survive the passing of the Badarian culture itself.

SPIRITUAL FORCES

Towards the end of the fifth millennium B.C., the Badarian culture gave way to the Nagada culture, so named after the village some twenty miles north of modern-day Luxor, where its remains were first recognized. (The culture has now been divided into three phases, I, II, III, spanning the entire fourth millennium B.C.). Some of the artifacts of the Nagada culture, most obviously the black-topped pottery and the slate palettes, have their ancestry in the previous Badarian period; some are distinctly new, such as the stone maceheads of Nagada I, and the buff wares with red-painted scenes of Nagada II.

But neither the Badarian nor the Nagada culture was literate. It was not until about 3100 B.C. that we have any evidence of writing in Egypt. Thereafter specific written evidence concerning Egyptian religious beliefs becomes increasingly frequent, and is abundant by 2400 B.C. Subsequently, until the collapse of pharaonic culture towards the end of the Roman era (*circa* fourth century A.D.), the development of Egyptian religious thought took many different paths. But we can best capture its essence at about 1400 B.C., from which time there survives a wealth of written and pictorial information from many different levels of society.

The Egyptians came to believe that there were a number of qualities which made up each individual, and that after death these qualities could enjoy a measure of independent existence. There was *sah*, the mummified corpse; *shuwt*, the shadow; *yib*, the heart; and most importantly, the elements of the personality, the *akh*, the *ka*, the *ba* together with the *ren*, the individual's name. The *akh* was that aspect which moved into the realm of the gods, to be part of the eternal movement of the stars. (This was a spiritual state attained only after one's worthiness had been demonstrated to the gods.) The *ka*, something akin to a "vital energy," which was created at birth, was the passive and re-

Illustration 1

Text Figure 1
KA-FIGURE OF TUTANKHAMUN
H., 1.69 m.
The Tomb of Tutankhamun, in the Valley of the Kings
1325 B.C.

This is one of two identical figures which flanked the sealed entrance to the burial chamber of Tutankhamun. The figures are of wood, overlaid in part with gilded plaster, and represent Tutankhamun himself, wearing a royal headdress, and carrying a staff in one hand and a royal mace in the other. Each figure is identified by an inscription as the *ka* of the king, so that they embody the force which provided him with life both before and after death. Since the *ka* was a protective being it is natural to find it guarding the vulnerable mummy in its chamber.

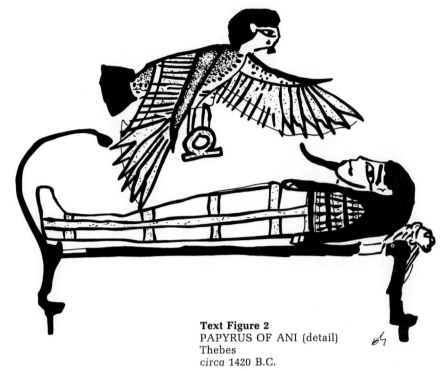

Text Figure 2
PAPYRUS OF ANI (detail)
Thebes
circa 1420 B.C.
This detail shows the *ba*-bird hovering over the mummy in the burial chamber.

mote double during life, but was re-united with an individual only after his death. It was the *ka* which required both foodstuffs and religious ritual for perpetuation of an afterlife. The *ba* represented the deceased with all physical powers—such as speech and movement—at their most fully developed. It is usually represented by the human-headed bird, and could leave the tomb during the day to wander at will. However, it normally would return at night to serve the needs of the mummified corpse, *sah*.

EGYPTIAN GODS

Presiding over all this spiritual activity was a complex hierarchy of gods, each with a different origin and festivals, a different cultic center, and sometimes with no more than a regional significance. Only a few of these gods were directly related to funeral ritual, but most were recorded at some point in the decoration of tombs or in associated texts. At the lowest level of the divine hierarchy there were popular gods usually responsible for either domestic activities or certain crafts. Bes, the dwarf-god guarding the tranquility of home,

and Tayet, the goddess of weaving, are amongst the better known of these. Next, there were powerful local gods, whose origins lay far in the past: they often attracted deep-rooted loyalties. Particularly popular among these were the cat-goddess, Bastet, from Bubastis in the Delta, and Khnum, the ram-god, from Aswan in the south.

Then, of greatest significance were the cosmic deities. Many of these controlled the basic forces of Nature, such as Geb, the earth-god, and Nut, the sky-goddess. As a group they maintained the proper order of life after the initial creation.

In particular, there was Re', the sun-god, who matured into a national deity out of a position of local significance at Heliopolis. His daily conquest of night's darkness represented the triumph of order over chaos. The stature of Re' in Egyptian religion was at its height around 2500 B.C., but in later times other divinities—notably Amun, the "hidden one"—joined him at the top of the divine structure.

However, by far the most important deity for our story is Osiris, the god of the Underworld. Initially associated with the city of Busiris in the Delta as a god of vegetation, he emerged quite suddenly around 2400 B.C. as a figure closely associated with the pharaoh, and then for the next twenty-seven hundred years reigned unchallenged as the ruler of the dead.

OSIRIS, THE COMPASSIONATE ONE

Osiris was the god of the dead, and to his worshippers, rich and poor, he promised resurrection after death. The inspiration for the faith with which he was honored was his own story of tragedy and ultimate triumph over the corruption and oblivion of death. The details of this story have not been preserved as such from any one coherent ancient Egyptian account, but can be reconstructed from allusions in literature, prayers, spells and other religious texts. In addition there is a Graeco-Roman myth that is quite complete and clear.

Osiris was once king of Egypt; he ruled wisely and well. But his brother Seth, envious of his power, struck him down and left him on the bank of the Nile. Osiris was found by his sisters, Isis and Nepthys, and they sat and wept over his dead body throughout the night. There followed a period of chaos in Egypt under Seth's rule, but it was during this time that Isis began to restore Osiris to life through embalming. Isis then conceived the child Horus by the revived Osiris.

When Seth heard of this birth he flew into a rage. Isis fled with the infant into the impenetrable marshes of the Delta and there nurtured him to manhood. Now Horus challenged Seth to recover his father's throne, and there ensued a legal wrangle in the tribunal of the gods, the proceedings of which were frequently disrupted by violent combats between the two contenders. Horus was the victor and, once he had assumed the throne, he was able to complete the rituals for the revitalization of his father. Thereafter Osiris assumed his full duties as god of the dead, the most important of which was to preside over the judgment of the individual's worthiness to attain eternal life.

There are numerous variations on the theme of this myth. By the end of the New Kingdom, it was believed that Seth not only killed Osiris but dismembered him, then scattered his remains throughout Egypt. Because of this, many towns laid claim to association with a relic of Osiris' body. (In keeping with the tradition of Abydos as the major cultic center for the god, it was here that the head was thought to have been buried.) Additionally, the Greek biographer Plutarch, early in the second century A.D., incorporated many notions not included in earlier sources of the myth. In this version Seth drowned Osiris, and the god's body was washed up at Byblos, far away on the coast of Lebanon. After Isis had contrived to bring the body back to Egypt, it was then that Seth dismembered it. Regardless of the differences in detail, all versions of the Osiris myth are both a religious drama and a device for fundamental moral instruction. The gift of Osiris was eternal life. At first this gift was available to the pharaoh alone, but, as we shall see, by 2000 B.C. it could be claimed by more of the population.

Illustration 5

II. MUMMIFICATION: THE EARLY PHASES

INTRODUCTION

Exactly why the practice of mummification developed in ancient Egypt remains obscure. In later historic periods the embalming of the body was ritually associated with the treatment accorded the body of Osiris, but this association cannot be traced further back than the textual appearance of Osiris himself rather late in the Old Kingdom (*circa* 2700-2250 B.C.).

However, the development of mummification can be charted through time quite satisfactorily on the basis of physical evidence alone. The earliest Egyptians buried their dead in simple pits dug in the sand,

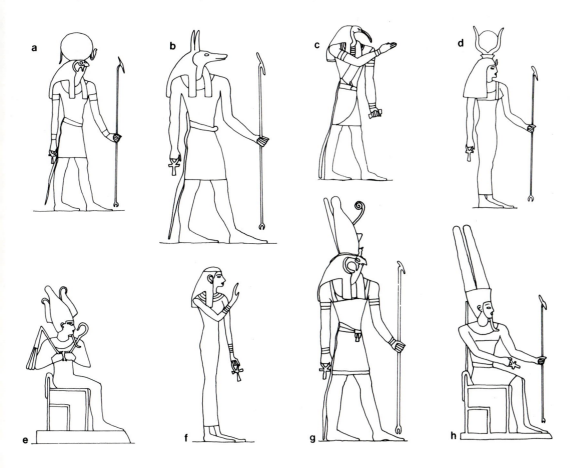

Text Figure 3
PRINCIPAL GODS OF ANCIENT EGYPT

a, Re', the sun-god; b, Anubis, god of embalming; c, Thoth, the scribe of the gods; d, Hathor, goddess of dancing and music; e, Osiris, god of the underworld; f, Isis, wife of Osiris; g, Horus, son of Osiris; and h, Amun-Re', the great state god and the principal god of the New Kingdom.

Text Figure 4
ROYAL TOMB OF THE 1ST DYNASTY
Abydos
circa 3000 B.C.

The burial chamber was a large open pit, subsequently roofed over, while the large, but simple, superstructure perhaps represents the primeval mound upon which the creator god stood when making the universe.

After W. Stevenson Smith, 1958: *The Art and Architecture of Ancient Egypt,* 25. (Penguin Books, Baltimore.)

without the use of any artificial means of preserving the corpse. Egypt's dry climate and intense summer heat created ideal conditions for natural dessication in the desert, so much so that some six thousand year old bodies still retain their facial characteristics. But this was not mummification.

It was only in the Archaic period (*circa* 3100-2700 B.C.) that there is evidence of the embalmers at work, initially with their use of elaborate linen bandaging that preserved the outline of the body. Then the body was laid in a wooden sarcophagus which was placed in a burial shaft, topped by a wooden roof. The tombs of pharaohs and nobles were more complex: they came to include a series of rooms for funerary goods—occasionally even a small-scale reconstruction of a granary—and a prominent mud-brick superstructure. It is in the impressive architecture of these tombs that we can see origins of the pyramid structures which develop in the Third Dynasty, *circa* 2700 B.C.

Unfortunately the body, royal or otherwise, was now isolated from the desert

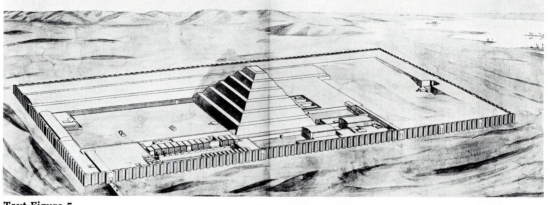

Text Figure 5
STEP PYRAMID OF DJOSER
Saqqara
3rd Dynasty, *circa* 2670 B.C.

The superstructure has become a great step pyramid in stone, combining perhaps the concepts of the primeval mound and a literal stairway to heaven for the deceased pharaoh. A funerary temple stood to the north, and a dummy royal palace surrounded the pyramid.

After J-P Lauer, 1936: *Fouilles à Saqqarah: La Pyramide à Degrés,* Plate IV. (L'Institut Français, Cairo.)

sand's capacity for natural preservation. Deeper graves did offer better protection against plunderers, the scavenging of jackals, and chance damage from violent storms. However, tomb dampness encouraged decay through bacterial attack on the flesh and body organs. Conditions were ripe for the first experiments with techniques of artificial preservation.

EARLY EMBALMING

By 2600 B.C., it became the practice to extract those organs most susceptible to rapid corruption: the lungs, liver, intestines and stomach. These were removed through an incision made in the left flank of the body, and placed in simple canopic jars, which were in turn placed in a plain stone chest. This chest was then placed in the tomb in a specially constructed niche.

It was around this time that the early embalmers began to use natron in their work. A mixture of sodium carbonate and sodium bicarbonate found naturally in several places throughout Egypt, natron is an unusually effective dessicant, indeed potentially more effective than desert sand. The earliest known evidence for the use of natron comes from remains in the canopic chest of Hetepheres, the mother of pharaoh Khufu, builder of the great pyramid at Giza (*circa* 2580 B.C.). But whether at this time natron was used in dry form (as became the rule in later periods) is unknown.

Regardless of the impact of these new techniques, the embalmers, by the end of the Fifth Dynasty (*circa* 2410 B.C.), encased the body in an elaborate linen and plaster shell modeled to reproduce the human form and painted with lifelike colors.

Somewhat later, some embalmers preferred to treat the body by pouring molten resin over it. This resin was derived from coniferous trees which grew in abundance in what is today Lebanon, and was transported to Egypt through the port of Byblos. (This area was also the source of the timber used for the better quality coffins of this period.) Despite the expense of importing it, the Egyptians considered the resin particularly desirable for the ritual purification of the deceased: they were fully familiar with its value as an incense. It was a fortunate by-product of this treatment that bacterial activity was suppressed by the molten resin on contact, and was subsequently inhibited by the sterile protective shell that was formed.

Throughout this initial phase of the history of embalming, mummification was a luxury reserved for the royal family and the highest nobility of the land. Few were offered the chance to promote their eternal existence through the preservation of the body, and this fact, coupled with the inadequacies of early embalming, is the principal reason why many questions at this stage in our story remain unanswered.

NEW ATTITUDES

By the beginning of the Sixth Dynasty (*circa* 2400 B.C.), it is clear that the central authority of the pharaoh was in decline. Regional governors did not attach the same value to a closeness to the royal court, and they tended more and more to build their tombs in their home region. After the death of Pepi II, about 2260 B.C., political anarchy ensued. For a further two decades, a few local rulers—particularly those at

Illustration 11

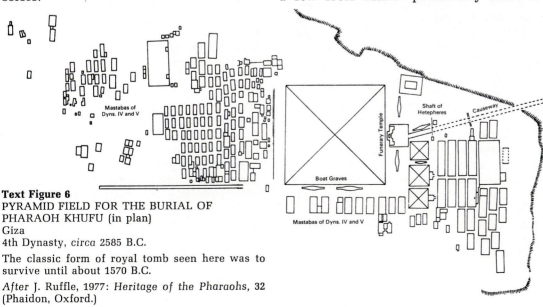

Text Figure 6
PYRAMID FIELD FOR THE BURIAL OF
PHARAOH KHUFU (in plan)
Giza
4th Dynasty, *circa* 2585 B.C.

The classic form of royal tomb seen here was to survive until about 1570 B.C.

After J. Ruffle, 1977: Heritage of the Pharaohs, 32
(Phaidon, Oxford.)

Illustration 16

Thinis, Dendereh, Assiut and Coptos—paid lip service to the pharaonic authority centered at the old royal capital of Memphis (close to modern Cairo). But increased regional hardship, aggravated by famine and civil strife, threw the country into turmoil. Psychologically as well as physically, Egypt returned to the state which it had known before its unification under Narmer a millennium before.

By about 2150 B.C., the situation had improved to a point where the squabbling provinces had coalesced into two rival kingdoms. A Tenth Dynasty crystallized at Heracleopolis in the north; an Eleventh Dynasty emerged at Thebes in the south. The following century was punctuated by brief outbreaks of war, but eventually the Thebans thrust northward to forcibly reunify the country and to found the Middle Kingdom (*circa* 2040-1780 B.C.).

This period of upheaval in Egypt's history is called the First Intermediate Period. It was characterized by a significant decline in all the material arts of civilization. The refined artistic products of the Old Kingdom workshops at Memphis and elsewhere were replaced by crude provincial versions. With the disappearance of skilled stone-masons and sculptors, combined with the breakdown of internal trade and regional inability to finance large quarrying operations, building in cut stone almost came to a halt. The dominant type of tomb for the upper classes was one cut roughly into the face of the cliff, with a simple façade opening into a spacious offering chapel decorated with painted scenes of daily life.

Illustration 15

Illustration 13

This change in tomb architecture is just one symptom of the general decline in the standard of living that occurred in the First Intermediate Period. Gold is less common in the graves, as are all imported luxury goods. At the same time, the privileges once accorded only to the highest level of society were now available to less illustrious, but still wealthy, individuals. This process of change, called democratization, resulted in a larger number of people being able to secure the tomb furnishings needed to provide for a well-equipped afterlife.

In the Old Kingdom, the Egyptians had hoped to transfer the most vital aspects of their earthly existence to their afterlife through the use of scenes sculpted onto the tomb wall, or by the inclusion of statuettes of servants engaged in domestic activities. Now, in the First Intermediate Period, this transfer was sought through wooden models, not just of servants but also of buildings and boats containing craftsmen, peasants and animals. For example, a whole carpenter's shop might be created inexpensively with painted figures only about four inches in height.

Along with the physical changes came changes in attitudes. The moral climate of the period is expressed in the so-called *Instructions for Merikare,* in which a pharaoh of the Tenth Dynasty advises his successor on the merits of restraint in the application of royal power and the importance of morality in government.

However, the most striking change was in the Egyptian attitude towards death. The nobles now held themselves equal to the pharaoh in that they too could expect eternal life and an identification with the revived Osiris. Versions of the spells once reserved solely for the pharaoh, and confined to the walls of the burial chamber of pyramids, begin to appear on the wooden coffins of the wealthy.

As for mummification in the First Intermediate Period, the following excerpt from the *Admonitions of Ipu-wer* is enlightening:

> . . . No one sails north to Byblos today. What can we do for pinetrees for our mummies? Pure Ones were buried by means of their produce, and prominent men were embalmed with their oils as far away as Crete. They [these products] do not come . . . (*Papyrus Leiden 344*)

Although this document was written about a hundred and fifty years after the events it describes, and represents a literary style which contains a certain degree of exaggeration, many of the conditions described in this excerpt can be confirmed by the archaeological record. The coffins are almost always made of local woods, and very few mummies have survived from the First Intermediate Period. So drastically was mummification affected that even the Eleventh Dynasty royal burials at Deir el-Bahri, of the subsequent Middle Kingdom period (beginning *circa* 2050 B.C.), displayed nothing like the care and attention which, centuries before, would have been considered essential.

1
BREAST COVER (DETAIL)
Cartonnage
L., 0.32 m.
Lahun
circa 200 B.C.

The rituals associated with mummification and burial were believed to be effective because they re-enacted the legend of Osiris, a king who was slain, dismembered, restored, and then revived through ritual to become the ruler of the dead. Many funerary artifacts reveal an equation between the deceased and Osiris that was thought to ensure that the deceased would be able to function in the afterlife. On this breast cover the mummy is shown lying on a lion-shaped funerary bier while Anubis (the jackal-headed god of embalming) applies ointments to it as part of the mummification process. Flanking this scene are Isis and Nepthys who reassembled and wrapped the dismembered body of Osiris. Overhead, the sky-goddess Nut extends her wings protectively over the mummification. She welcomes the spirits of the dead when they ascend to the sky, but she also symbolizes the orderly universe in which the sky, air, land and all other elements have a proper place. (To indicate this, Nut clasps feathers representing Maat, the goddess of order and balance.) Through mummification and ritual the corpse became an entity, the *sah,* able to function in the afterlife, but always confined to the burial chamber.

(University Museum: E352)

2
OSTRACON BEARING THE SKETCH OF A *BA*-BIRD
Limestone
L., 0.15 m.
Thebes
circa 1200 B.C.

The mummy itself could not leave the burial chamber but from about 2000 B.C. onwards the Egyptians believed that the dead man could assume the form of a *ba,* a human-headed bird. Since the *ba* was mobile it could fly up the tomb shaft, partake of the offerings in the tomb chapel, and fly out into the sunlight so that the deceased could experience once more the basic pleasures of the living. At sunset the myriads of *ba* were imagined as fluttering into the tombs, so as to descend into the underworld with the sun-god Re,' and not be exposed to the dangers of the night.

(University Museum: E1884)

3

INSCRIPTION OF HETEP-HER-AKHET
H., 1.6 m.
Giza, carved on one side of the entrance to the deceased's tomb chapel of his mastaba
5th Dynasty, *circa* 2450 B.C.

> The elder Judge of the Hall, Hetep-her-akhet, says: I made this tomb on the west side in a pure place, in which there was no tomb of anyone, in order to protect the possession of one who has gone to his *ka*. As for any people who would enter this tomb unclean and do something evil to it, there will be a judgment against them by the great god. I made this tomb because I was honoured by the king, who brought me a sarcophagus. (M. Lichtheim, 1975: vol. 1, p. 16)

This Fifth Dynasty text contains one of the earliest references to the *ka,* at a time when a private person, unlike the pharaoh, was thought to be separated from his *ka* during life. Here Hetep-her-akhet stresses his care not to intrude into the area of older tombs. Such intrusion had already become commonplace and had caused serious distortions in the carefully planned cemeteries of the Fourth Dynasty.

(Courtesy of the Rijksmuseum van Oudheden, Léiden)

4

OFFERING TABLE
Sandstone
H., 0.45 m.
Nubia
Meroitic Period (*circa* 270 B.C. - A.D. 320)

According to ancient Egyptian funerary beliefs, the provision of sustenance for the deceased was essential. To that end, from the Old Kingdom onwards, offering slabs or tables were placed within the chapel, or at the entrance to the tomb, so that the deceased's *ka* could receive gifts of foodstuffs to sustain it in the afterlife. These slabs were sometimes in the shape of a hieroglyph which represented a loaf placed upon a reed mat. Libation vessels, loaves of bread, joints of beef, and so on, were often carved in relief upon these tables to ensure these provisions to the deceased in the event that the funerary cult failed to provide the actual items. The tables were also provided with a basin or depression, into which water or other liquid could be poured. The names and titles of the deceased as well as the standard offering formulae were frequently inscribed upon the tables.

This example was found at the entrance to a tomb not in Egypt but in Nubia, the land to the south of Egypt which was greatly influenced by Egyptian culture. It dates to the Meroitic Period (*circa* 270 B.C. - A.D. 320), a time during which an independent kingdom was maintained, with its capital at Meroe. The inscription at the edge of the table is therefore written in the Meroitic script rather than in Egyptian hieroglyphs. Loaves of bread and libation vessels are clustered around the cartouche-shaped depression.

(University Museum: E7089)

5

FRAGMENT OF A STATUE
Basalt
H., 0.21 m.
Provenance uncertain, probably Memphis
circa 600 B.C.

The statue represents an unidentified man holding a figure of Osiris. The god is shown in a character-istic mummy form, holding a crook and flail, and wearing a plumed crown.

The legend of Osiris described how he was an an-cient king, slain and dismembered by his envious brother Seth, but later restored and revitalized by the acts of Nepthys, Isis and Horus. Osiris became god of the dead and funerary rituals frequently re-ferred to his legend.

The cult of Osiris rose to prominence in the late Old Kingdom. The pharaoh, identified with Horus during his lifetime, became Osiris in death. Grad-ually, over time, this equivalence to Osiris was ex-tended to include Egyptian people of all classes who were buried with proper ritual.

Osiris was also the god of vegetation. His death and resurrection were mirrored by the cycle of the seasons, particularly the annual inundation of the Nile and the subsequent productivity of the sur-rounding land.

(University Museum: E14313)

6

ISIS NURSING HORUS
Bronze
H., 0.27 m.
Provenance uncertain, possibly Saqqara
Late Period, *circa* 575 B.C.

The myth of Isis nursing her infant son Horus was a popular one in later times. Isis was impregnated by the deceased Osiris after his body had been reassembled. When Horus was born Isis raised him in the seclusion of the marshes of the Delta (thus hiding themselves from Seth) until he was mature enough to deal with his father's murderer. During this period divine powers were invoked by Isis to protect Horus from venomous insects and harmful animals, so the image of Isis nursing Horus was regarded as a powerful, protective one.

(University Museum: E14293)

7
HORUS AND SETH IN COMBAT
Edfu, relief on the Temple of Horus
1st century B.C.

The best preserved of all Egyptian temples is that of Horus at Edfu. It depicts many incidents in the struggle between Horus and Seth over the throne of Egypt. Here Horus, aided by his mother Isis, spears Seth, who is represented as a hippopotamus.

In the late version of the Osiris myth as represented at Edfu, Seth is described as a red hippopotamus who, with a following of crocodiles, fled from Horus down the Nile, from Aswan to Edfu. At Edfu, Horus hurled ten harpoons at the beast, and destroyed him. The hippopotamus was dismembered amid much celebration, while Horus was confirmed in his victory by a divine tribunal.

By this time in Egyptian history, Seth was considered the embodiment of chaos, and was often associated with the foreigners who had humiliated Egypt. He is therefore represented at Edfu on a diminutive scale, in contrast with the majestic stature of Horus.

(Courtesy of B. Fishman, Oriental Institute, Chicago)

8
OXYRHYNCHUS FISH
Bronze
L., 0.12 m.
Provenance uncertain, possibly Thebes
4th century B.C. or later

This gray-colored fish, formally named *Marymus kannume*, is to be found the length of the Nile below Lake Victoria. It has been identified in temple inscriptions as a manifestation of the goddess Hathor (who often wore the crown, with a horned sun-disc, that this bronze statuette bears), and was thus a sacred creature.

However, the fish itself is important in one of the later versions of the Osiris legend, as it reputedly swallowed the god's phallus. This part of Osiris' anatomy was thus denied to Isis and Nepthys when they sought to collect and reconstitute the dismembered parts of Osiris and revive him.

(University Museum: 54-33-6)

9

**RELIEF DEDICATED TO A WOMAN NAMED
SENEB-ES AND A MAN NAMED MER-ANKH-EF**
Limestone
H., 0.55 m.
Provenance uncertain, possibly Giza
Early 5th Dynasty, *circa* 2500 B.C.

This relief is a tablet from a "false door" included in the structure of an Old Kingdom tomb as a doorway from the afterworld. In it would stand a figure similar to Khenu (see 12). The couple are seated before an offering table heaped with bread, beer, linen, alabaster, incense, malachite eye-cosmetic, and oils.

Seneb-es held the title king's acquaintance; Mer-ankh-ef is identified as ruler of the estate.

The most interesting feature of this piece is the placement of the female on the left side in the usually dominant position. We unfortunately do not know the relationship of the couple, but she is presumably his wife or mother. It is clear though that the false door was manufactured for Mer-ankh-ef, since hieroglyphs which comprise the offerings almost invariably face in the direction of the deceased for whom the tablet was intended. Only four parallels for this figure arrangement are known, all from tombs at Giza.

(University Museum: 29-209-1)

10

BURIAL CHAMBER OF HETEPHERES
Giza
circa 2580 B.C.

The rich funerary goods of the royal builders of the Old Kingdom pyramids have not survived, but in 1925 the Boston-Harvard expedition, under George Reisner, discovered at Giza the apparently intact tomb of Queen Hetepheres, mother of the builder of the Great Pyramid, the pharaoh Khufu. The deep rock-cut shaft and chamber tomb had a carefully concealed entrance and contained an alabaster coffin, some valuable jewelry, several large pieces of furniture, wooden boxes containing linen, stone vases, much pottery, and other items. The boxes had decayed, and their contents had fallen into an extraordinary jumble. In the southwest corner, illustrated here, we see the coffin on the left; placed on it are the disassembled parts of a wooden bed-canopy overlaid with gold sheeting. On the right, decayed linen, stone vases and broken pottery lie tumbled together.

The careful recording of this tomb took more than a year, but at the end the coffin proved to be empty. Apparently Hetepheres' original tomb had been partially robbed and her body destroyed; her burial equipment was subsequently placed in this secret tomb near her son's pyramid. In a niche was a canopic box containing remains of natron, showing that artificial mummification was already being practiced at this early date.

(Courtesy of the Museum of Fine Arts, Boston)

11
THE MUMMY OF WATY
Saqqara, Tomb of Nefer
5th Dynasty, *circa* 2470 B.C.

Waty, a singer and writer of lyrics, was buried in a shaft of the east wall of the tomb of Nefer, at Saqqara. The body was tightly swathed in linen strips and impregnated with light green stucco plaster. The form of the face was fully detailed in the plaster's surface, as were a narrow moustache, long-arched eye-brows, and a ceremonial beard of stiff linen.

The wall paintings in the tomb (built *circa* 2490 B.C.) record the success of Nefer, initially as a court singer, then as confidant to the pharaoh Niuser-re'. Shafts close to the west wall, now damaged and empty, were once the resting places for not only Nefer's immediate family but also that of his brother, Wer-bauw. Waty appears to have been a friend of the family. The survival of this mummy, the oldest intact yet found *in situ,* was a fortunate consequence of the construction of a raised walkway for funeral processions, instigated by the pharaoh Unas when building his pyramid complex some sixty years after Waty's death. Tomb robbers had moved swiftly to steal the statuary that would have been placed in a niche of the chapel above the burial shafts, and the workmen had stripped out much of the stone of the main group of graves. But, as the builders moved on, Waty's burial was soon completely sealed by tons of debris and the gradual drift of dry desert sand into the tomb chamber.

(Courtesy of *The Sunday Times,* London)

12
THE *KA*-STATUE OF KHENU
Limestone
H., 0.84 m.
Saqqara
5th Dynasty, *circa* 2450 B.C.

While extraordinary efforts were made to create life-like mummies in the Old Kingdom, the offering cult in the chapel that was provided above ground for the tomb was focused on images of the deceased. These images were carved or painted on the chapel walls, or often were free-standing. The statue of Khenu, an official of the Fifth Dynasty buried at Saqqara near the royal capital of Memphis, is an outstanding example of such funerary art. The statue was believed to embody Khenu's *ka,* the life-force which enabled him to function both in life and after death, and represented Khenu himself. However, like most Egyptian statues, it was not a true portrait, the inscribing of Khenu's name on the base being sufficient to establish its identity. The *ka* was imagined to enter the chapel from the tomb *via* a carved false door; hence the striding forward position of the statue. For security, however, Khenu's *ka*-statue was probably placed in a *serdab,* a hidden chamber adjoining the offering chapel.

(University Museum: E14301)

13
COFFIN OF THE GOVERNMENT OFFICIAL, AHA-NAKHT
Wood
L., 2.58 m.
el-Bersheh
First Intermediate Period, *circa* 2000 B.C.

The coffin of Aha-Nakht was made of thick planks of coniferous wood, and decorated on the exterior with a band of hieroglyphs near the upper part. Carved and painted, these hieroglyphs read from right to left, and express an offering formula typical for this period. Visible is the expression: "A gift that the king gives and Osiris, Lord of Busiris, Foremost of the Westerners, Great God, Lord of Festivals; may invocation offerings go forth for the revered one, the count, controller of the two seats, Aha-Nakht, justified." On the far side, it is possible to see part of another invocation and there the deceased is "revered before Anubis." Carved underneath the band of hieroglyphs in a rectangle is a pair of wadjet eyes which will enable Aha-Nakht to see out (see 35).

(University Mueum: E16218)

14
INTERIOR OF THE COFFIN OF AHA-NAKHT
Wood
L., 0.93 m.
el-Bersheh
First Intermediate Period, *circa* 2000 B.C.

The decoration on the inside of the coffin consists of a frieze of objects, painted in a horizontal band near the top, representing the necessities the deceased would use in the afterlife. In vertical columns are signs carved in a cursive form of hieroglyphs. Similar to the script used primarily for writing on papyri, these signs lack inner detail and are quite abbreviated forms of the hieroglyphs. As is the case with many contemporaneous coffins, these columns of writing comprise a group of spells called the Coffin Texts. Composed of some spells originating in the Pyramid Texts, others which are derived from the same source, but altered or edited, a few spells which eventually become chapters of the New Kingdom "Book of the Dead," and still others that appear to be specific to the Coffin Texts,

these writings were meant to protect the deceased as he enters his afterlife, ensure success in this endeavor, and prepare him for his identification with the immortal ones. Such funerary literature had been reserved for pharaohs in the Old Kingdom, but it was democratized during the First Intermediate Period to include wealthy members of society, such as Aha-Nakht.

Although oriented right to left (i.e., the figures always face toward the beginning of the text), the text is read from left to right; such "retrograde" writing is not uncommon among funerary and magical texts. Part of the rather long Spell 75 occurs in much of the inscription, but each column represents only part of what was originally written. This spell deals with the air-god Shu and the identification of the deceased with him as well as with other gods: "This Aha-Nakht is in the midst of this circle, the Lord of Fields; this Aha-Nakht, may he appear as Osiris."

(University Museum: E16218)

13

14

15
FUNERARY STELA OF NEFERSEFEKHY
Limestone
H., 0.58 m.
Nag'el-Deir
First Intermediate Period, *circa* 2175 B.C.

In content and style, this stela is typical of its period. The first two horizontal lines contain an offering invocation to Anubis and identify the stela's owner, Nefersefekhy, as an official and priest of the town of Thinis in Middle Egypt. In the third and fourth horizontal lines, Nefersefekhy boasts of his virtues and self-reliance, that make him superior to all other Thinites of the same rank and that have enabled him to provide for his brothers and sisters. These individualistic, biographical remarks typically replace those which would have been used in the Old Kingdom, referring to service to the kingship (an institution now in eclipse) rather than to one-self.

The vertical panels list a series of offerings, some of which are depicted below, being brought to the large figure of Nefersefekhy on the left. (He wears a priestly leopard skin over his linen clothing.) The bold and eccentric forms of the hieroglyphs, and the marked stylization which replaces the more realistic style of the Old Kingdom in the depiction of people and animals, are characteristic of the First Intermediate Period.

(University Museum: 40-19-1)

16
MODEL BOAT
Wood
L. 0.74 m.
Sedment (Middle Egypt)
First Intermediate Period, *circa* 2510 B.C.

The democratization of funerary beliefs and customs in the First Intermediate Period inspired many less well-off Egyptians to create representations of their daily environment which they believed would continue into the afterlife. Unable to afford the scenes carved and painted on the funerary chapel and tomb chamber walls of wealthier Egyptians, poorer indi-viduals purchased models representing various aspects of daily life and placed them in the tomb shaft or in the burial chamber with the other funerary gifts. These models included miniature granaries, butcher's yards, carpenter's shops and weaving establishments, all imagined to be producing food and goods for the deceased. Boats were the main means of long term traveling in Egypt, so boat models were frequent. Since boats were used to make pilgrimages to holy places, like the Osiris cult center at Abydos, boat models also have a religious significance.

(University Museum: E14260)

III. THE MARRIAGE OF RITUAL AND TECHNOLOGY

With the opening of the Middle Kingdom under Mentuhotep II, trade links were re-established with the Mediterranean lands, and with those African peoples to the south. The renewed vigor of a re-united Egypt is demonstrated by the scale of quarrying expeditions undertaken by Mentuhotep III and Mentuhotep IV at Wadi Hammamat to the east of Thebes. The control of the throne was abruptly seized by Amunemhet, Mentuhotep IV's chief official, *circa* 1990 B.C. (to begin the Twelfth Dynasty), but this does not appear to have interrupted the central government's growth in prosperity. Indeed the two centuries that followed were amongst the most productive in ancient Egypt, in both an economic and a cultural sense.

Once more the embalmers found full employment. In a passage from the famous Middle Kingdom *Story of Sinuhe*, the pharaoh Senwosret I urges Sinuhe, a self-proclaimed fugitive from the court, to return to Egypt and consider the benefits of a proper Egyptian funeral as opposed to the primitive manner of burial available in Syria at this time:

... Indeed, today old age has begun for you ... Remember for yourself the day of burial, when one attains veneration. The night shall be appointed for you with coniferous oil, and wrappings from the arms of Tayet. A funeral procession shall be made for you on the day of burial, the coffins [overlaid] with gold and the head with lapis lazuli ... you will be placed on the sledge, oxen dragging you, singers preceding you ... You shall not die in a foreign land ... Asiatics will not escort you; you shall not be placed in the skin of a ram when your coffin is made ... *Berlin Papyrus* 3022).

The embalmers of the Middle Kingdom

Text Figure 7
"MARSH LIFE"
Saqqara; scene from the Tomb chapel of the nobleman, Mereruka
6th Dynasty, *circa* 2350 B.C.

The river and its fringes of marsh lands were favorite places of recreation for the nobility, and an important source of food. In the upper register of this scene rowers, with garlands on their heads, move skiffs across the water; beneath, fish of various kinds are carried as offerings; and, in the lowest register, men engage in the dangerous sport of harpooning hippopotami.

After P. Duell, 1938: *The Mastaba of Mereruka,* plate 13. (The University of Chicago, Oriental Institute Publ. XXXI.)

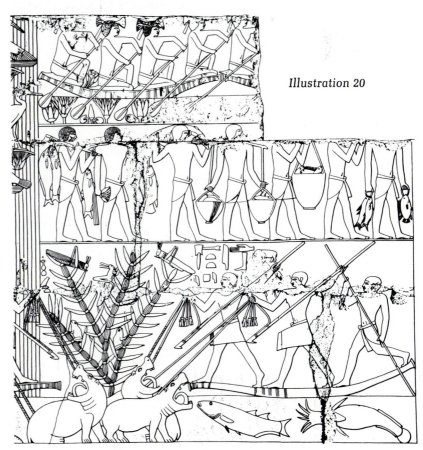

Illustration 20

(*circa* 2050-1780 B.C.) continued to gut the body of the internal organs when preparing for more elaborate burials. The removed organs were again stored in canopic jars, but these were now provided with stoppers in the form of human heads. There seems to have been a need for a cheaper (or at least more simple) procedure, so that we now find many examples where the evisceration step is simply dropped. The embalmer then relied on natron's dessication powers alone. For example, this treatment, together with an application of various gum resins, was given the family members of Mentuhotep II. The drying procedure seems to have been incomplete, for the bodies were still moist when bandaged, and continued to decay after wrapping.

An additional variation on conventional embalming methods—perhaps a unique one—was the treatment of some sixty of Mentuhotep's soldiers buried in a common tomb cut roughly in the cliffs at Deir el-Bahri. Not even natron was used; instead the uneviscerated bodies were merely dried (probably in the sand, some of which still clings to their skin), then carefully wrapped in linen. These mummies, too, subsequently decayed extensively. Only two of the soldiers were provided with coffins.

In wealthy burials coffins were of vital importance, not only for their practical function but also as a magical aid. This is because many funerary spells were written on the interior of the coffins, close to the body. Typical of these spells is the following:

The members of Osiris are inert, but they shall not be inert, they shall not putrefy or shake, nor swell up or make foul liquid. O you who come from the acacia tree of the Double Lion, to Horus in the midst of his corruption, may you (?) come and see me at the house of Him who approaches his father (?). Say: Do not choke in this your name of Him of Oxyrhynchus; do not putrefy in this your name of Ha; do not decay in this your name of Anubis; do not drip on the ground in this your name of Jackal. (R. O. Faulkner, 1977; vol. II, p. 288, for Spell 755)

Such a spell was meant to insure the body's integrity and capacity to function. Once this was accomplished, the deceased would then use other spells to prepare for the next stage in the journey to eternity. He would marshall his powers (identifying them with those of the gods), familiarize himself with spells which would compel obedience to his wishes, and demonstrate his full awareness of the geography of the underworld. He could now confidently face an obstacle course of demons, guardians of the gateways, and inquisitors, who lay between him and immortality:

As for any man who is seen yonder alive, he will never perish since he knows the spells of those who squat, the keepers of the gates. (R. O. Faulkner, 1978; vol. III, p. 147, for Spell 1081)

Through these coffin texts we can trace the progress of democratization in the fun-

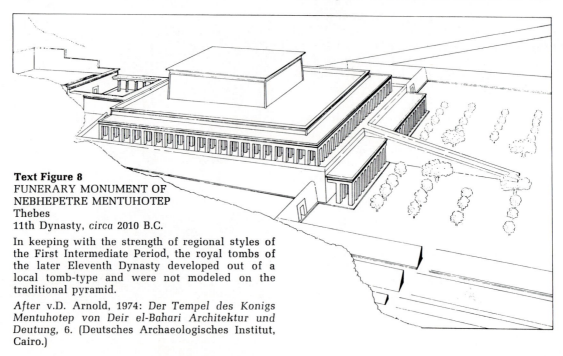

Text Figure 8
FUNERARY MONUMENT OF
NEBHEPETRE MENTUHOTEP
Thebes
11th Dynasty, *circa* 2010 B.C.

In keeping with the strength of regional styles of the First Intermediate Period, the royal tombs of the later Eleventh Dynasty developed out of a local tomb-type and were not modeled on the traditional pyramid.

After v.D. Arnold, 1974: Der Tempel des Konigs Mentuhotep von Deir el-Bahari Architektur und Deutung, 6. (Deutsches Archaeologisches Institut, Cairo.)

eral practices of ancient Egypt, since many of the texts have their origins in spells which were once available to pharaohs alone, and were carved only in the inner chambers of their pyramids. There is the difference that pyramid texts convey only those notions of afterlife which were held by royalty, whereas coffin texts give us a far more detailed insight into how the afterlife was viewed by the literate population as a whole. Common to both sets of funerary texts, however, was the belief that, together with mummification, they were essential for entrance to eternity.

NATIONAL HUMILIATION

The close of the Twelfth Dynasty ushered in a period of internal collapse and foreign invasion known as the Second Intermediate Period. Now pharaoh succeeded pharaoh with alarming frequency, so that reigns as short as four months are recorded. With royal prestige and power at their lowest ebb, the reins of government fell into the hands of highly placed officials. For a while the maintenance of a central government ensured Egypt's reputation abroad, but it was only a matter of time before Semitic peoples, called the Hyksos, took over the royal capital of Memphis. From about 1670 B.C. onwards, the Hyksos exercised control over the length of the Nile. This was a humiliation the Egyptians never forgot, and a century after the Hyksos had been expelled they recalled Hyksos rule as a symbol of loathsome chaos.

In the south the native Egyptian rulers chafed under this foreign domination and continuously conspired against the Hyksos. The Egyptians retained the freedom to pursue traditional forms of religious practices, including mummification, but the growing intensity of military conflict was highly disruptive of trading along the Nile. The imported materials essential for embalming could not reach the Thebans. Consequently, the mummies from this, the late Seventeenth Dynasty—including that of pharaoh Sekenenre' II—were roughly prepared and do not seem to have been treated with the usual coniferous resins.

Illustration 21

Consistent with the lack of national confidence at this time, there was a clear change in the religious atmosphere. This can be illustrated by a song from a funerary banquet inscribed in the tomb chapel of pharaoh Intef, that expresses doubt about the very existence of the afterlife:

... those who built tombs, their places have gone, what has become of them? ... None comes from there to tell of their needs, to calm our hearts, until we go where they have gone! ... [so] make holiday, and do not weary of it. Lo, none is allowed to take his goods with him; lo, none who depart come back again! ... (M. Lichtheim, 1975, Vol. 1, pp. 196-197, from *Papyrus Harris* 500)

Text Figure 9
TOMB OF AN ASIATIC (HYKSOS) WARRIOR
(in plan)
Tell ed Dab'a, in the eastern Delta
Second Intermediate Period, *circa* 1600 B.C.

The burial gifts, and customs such as the burial of sacrificial animals with the deceased, are Palestinian, not Egyptian in character.

After M. Bietak, 1968: Mitteilungen des Deutschen Archaeologischen Instituts Abteilung Kairo 23, **91** (Otto Harrassowitz, Wiesbaden.)

Text Figure 10
TOMB OF SETI I (in section)
Valley of the Kings
19th Dynasty, *circa* 1280 B.C.

This is the largest of the royal tombs at Thebes.
The section indicates the deep drainage pit at the
end of the first two slopes, and the attempt to
stop robbery by concealment of the continuation
of the passage beneath a false floor in the first
chamber.

After J. Ruffle, 1977: Heritage of the Pharaohs, 67
(Phaidon, Oxford.)

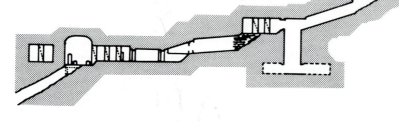

NEW RULERS, NEW IDEAS

Illustration 29

After a series of campaigns by Sekenenre'
II and his son Kamose, the Hyksos power
was confined to just a small portion of the
northeastern region of the Delta. Then
Kamose's brother, Ahmose, succeeded in
forcing the invaders out of Egypt completely, and chased them into Palestine.
With Ahmose begins the Eighteenth Dynasty (*circa* 1570-1293 B.C.) and a renewed
growth in the economic wealth and prestige
of Egypt, which was to continue throughout the next two dynasties until the close
of the New Kingdom in 1070 B.C.

Illustration 33

Now, instead of erecting great pyramids,
the pharaohs after Amunhotep I chose to
hide their burials among the rugged cliffs in
the desolate area just to the north of Deir
el-Bahri (western Thebes), known today as
the Valley of the Kings. (Implicit in this
move was a desire to frustrate tomb robbers attracted by the immense wealth now
committed to royal burials.) A separate
pyramid was no longer built for each tomb,
but the great peak of western Thebes represented a natural pyramid. The royal funerary temples were built along its eastern
foot. In all, some forty royal tombs (and a
few non-royal ones) were clustered together here, including that of Seti I (who
died in 1279 B.C.), with its complex ground-
plan, superlative wall decoration and re-
nowned astronomical ceiling.

Illustration 25

The process of democratization of funeral privilege now moves forward smoothly
to cover a prosperous middle class of minor
court officials, civil servants, lower orders
of the priesthood, and highly skilled artisans. The pyramid, in small scale, was now
adopted for private individuals, the tombs
themselves often serving as family vaults.

The art of embalming was also fast ap-
proaching its peak of quality, with the important exception (among royal burials) of
the mummy of Tutankhamun, which was
badly burnt by the excessive use of
resins.

It was now a matter of routine for the
brain to be removed from the skull, by
breaking the ethmoid bone inside the nose
and drawing the cerebral matter out
through the nostrils by means of a hooked
probe. Usually the skull was now left
empty, but in the wealthier burials it might
be filled with resin. The treatment of the
internal organs did not differ markedly
from that of earlier periods although a
great deal of variety can be seen in the
types of materials with which the eviscerated body was packed. As before, the
removed organs were placed in canopic
jars, the human-headed lids of the Middle
Kingdom being replaced by ones representing the heads of the Four Sons of Horus.
These were protective deities, the stomach
being guarded by the jackal-headed Duamutef; the intestines by the hawk-headed
Kebehsenuef; the lungs by the ape-headed
Hapy; and the liver and gall bladder by the
human-headed Imsety. (As in all periods in
the history of embalming, the heart was
left in the body, since it was regarded as
the center of intelligence and was required
to play an important role after death in the
judgment of the deceased's moral worth.)
Later in the New Kingdom it became common to use linen pads and resin-soaked
bandage rolls to fill out the shape of the
eviscerated corpse, and to tone the skin's
surface with ocher pigments: traditionally
red for men, yellow for women.

Perhaps the most crucial period of New Kingdom history was the reign of the pharaoh Akhenaten (1350-1334 B.C.) that, for a brief time, altered almost every aspect of Egyptian cultural achievement. Whereas the Egyptians of previous periods had been content to emphasize the supremacy of one among their many gods (such as Re' in the Old Kingdom, and Amun subsequently), Akhenaten sought to suppress the existence of other gods in favor of Aten, the sun disc. The worship of Osiris and its related funeral practices were de-emphasized. In Akhenaten's tomb at his royal capital of Tell el Amarna, there is no underworld god or demon to be seen, no text to guide the pharaoh to his afterlife.

Although it was an Osirian practice, mummification persisted. This pharaoh's mother, queen Tiye, was embalmed in the most expensive manner, and even though Akhenaten's body itself may not have survived, the existence of his canopic chest indicates he too was mummified.

Akhenaten had imposed his novel religious changes upon a reluctant people, so that after his death all the principal elements of the old religious ideas quickly reasserted themselves. Only ten years later they are fully expressed in the vast wealth and complexity of the funerary equipment of Tutankhamun. However, from this time forward, we can detect some subtle shifts of attitude. Cheerful scenes of daily life which were once a feature of Theban tombs became less common, and tended to be replaced by scenes and texts which dwelt upon the activities and perils of the afterlife.

Though the majority of the people still fervently hoped for, and prepared for, a full renewal in their afterlife, evidence of individual loss of faith became more pronounced:

. . . How sad is the descent in the land of Silence. The wakeful sleeps, he who did not slumber at night lies still forever. The scorners say: the dwelling place of the inhabitants of the West is deep and dark. It has no door, no window, no light to illuminate it, no north wind to refresh the heart. The sun does not rise there, but they lie every day in darkness . . . Those who are in the

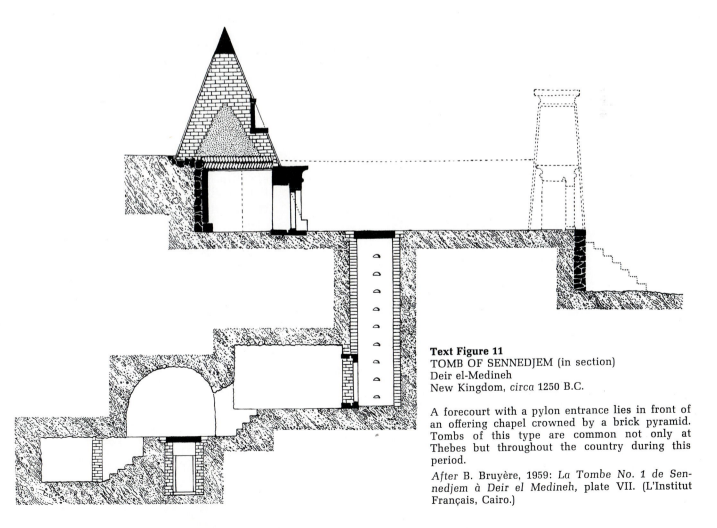

Text Figure 11
TOMB OF SENNEDJEM (in section)
Deir el-Medineh
New Kingdom, *circa* 1250 B.C.

A forecourt with a pylon entrance lies in front of an offering chapel crowned by a brick pyramid. Tombs of this type are common not only at Thebes but throughout the country during this period.

After B. Bruyère, 1959: *La Tombe No. 1 de Sennedjem à Deir el Medineh*, plate VII. (L'Institut Français, Cairo.)

Illustration 37

West are cut off, and their existence is misery. One is loathe to go and join them. (H. Kees in H. Frankfort, 1961, p. 108, from the tomb of Nefersekheru at Kom el-Ahmar.)

MAGICAL DEFENCES

Illustration 40

During the New Kingdom a complex mixture of morality and magic dominated the funeral ritual. For example, starting in the Eighteenth Dynasty a popular concept frequently illustrated in funerary papyri was the weighing of the heart against the goddess Maat (symbolizing truth, justice and harmony) in the presence of Osiris. If the heart did not exactly balance Maat, it testified that the deceased had sinned while alive, and the individual would be denied an afterlife, and all his funeral preparations would have been in vain. However, this fate could be avoided if a scarab or a heart-shaped amulet bearing the correct spell was worn on the chest of the mummy. This would prevent the heart from revealing any of its owner's moral failings.

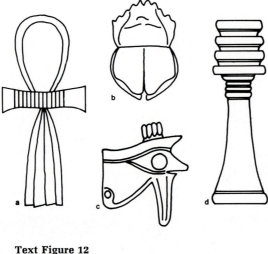

Text Figure 12
TRADITIONAL AMULETS

a, *ankh;* b, scarab beetle; c, *wadjet* eye; and d, *djed*-pillar.

Magical spells were now relied upon to overcome *every* obstacle on the path to the afterlife. These spells were conveniently brought together on single rolls of papyrus to be buried close to the deceased in his coffin. The Egyptians called such papyri *Peret-kheru* or "The going forth by day"; today they are commonly called "The Book of the Dead." One version of "The Book of the Dead" is not necessarily like another, and the quality of their workmanship is highly variable. The basic corpus of spells numbered just under two hundred, and of these a large or small selection would be written out on the papyrus roll, the text being accompanied by scenes depicting the afterlife.

To complement this funeral literature there was an increase in the use of amulets. As before, many were based on hieroglyphs representing words which already had a long history in the Egyptian religion: for example the *ankh* (which meant life), the scarab beetle (which meant transformation and rebirth), the *wadjet* eye (which meant health and revitalization) and the *djed*-pillar (which meant permanence and stability of existence). Others were miniature images of deities (for example, Sakhmet, goddess of war and disease) the possession of which would protect the deceased. Still others, such as pylon-shaped plaques decorated with images of funerary deities, are quite new.

This increased use of amulets and this far heavier dependence upon the power of funerary papyri reveal the increasing availability to Egyptians in general of the means of ensuring for themselves a successful afterlife, a privilege previously limited to the royal family and the nobility. These changes also mark a strong reliance upon magic rather than upon moral behavior. In the Old Kingdom, adherence to a moral code while the individual was alive was perhaps regarded as a basic requirement for admission into the afterlife; by the New Kingdom, the use of magic made morally correct behavior less necessary.

IV. FUNERAL RITUAL

CULTIC CENTERS

By the end of the Eighteenth Dynasty (*circa* 1300 B.C.), the worship of Osiris had become by far the most popular national religious cult. One stela, dedicated by the government official Amunmose, cites no less than nine cult centers for this god, running from Busiris in the Delta to Abydos in Upper Egypt. Abydos was the most important of these, and, as such, featured an annual play re-enacting the dramatic events of the Osiris story. Since the Middle Kingdom, and perhaps even before, Abydos had been a place of pilgrimage for Egyptians seeking a stronger association with Osiris. Indeed, some sought to have their tombs erected on the sacred ground, while others had to be content with a memorial shrine there.

Some one hundred miles to the south, at Thebes, many tombs of great beauty were cut into the cliffs and the tomb walls were covered with scenes of the deceased enjoying activities of daily life. Often also there were scenes detailing the events of the funeral itself, and it is from these that we can reconstruct the way in which the deceased was laid to rest some thirty-five hundred years ago.

THE LAST JOURNEY

The prudent Egyptian man of wealth began the preparation for his death while still in the prime of his life. First he would cross the Nile to the western bank where he would select a site in the sprawling Theban cemetery. Then, a few years of work might be devoted to the cutting of the tomb; several years would be devoted to its decoration. At the same time, work on individual items of funerary furniture would begin: the coffin itself (which would then have to be elaborately decorated), the canopic jars and their chest, the sled used in the funeral procession, and the principal statuary, such as the *ka* figure and the offering stela. Other crucial items, such as the "Book of the Dead" would then be commissioned. The expense of preparing the tomb and its associated equipment was usually a private matter, although certain favored individuals might be lent the services of royal workmen and artists for short periods of time. Ideally, all the decoration was finished and the bulkiest of the tomb furnishings were already in place long before the day of burial.

When death finally came, the deceased would be taken to the embalmer's shop for the lengthy process of mummification. As a rule, some seventy days were allotted to this task, thus leaving ample time for completion of the funerary preparations. Now the minor items, such as boxes, baskets, and jars to be used for the storage of food, drink and oils were gathered. Representative items were selected from among the deceased's personal possessions and made ready.

Then, on the day of the funeral, the mummy in its coffin would be placed on a sled, while groups of relatives and friends (many of them wearing ritual clothing) were gathering at the house of the deceased. Oxen were hitched to the sled and the funeral procession would form about it, with a *sem*-priest at the front, holding an incense burner and ritually purifying the path of the cortege with sprinklings of milk. Behind the sled itself would follow groups of wailing women not only family but also professional mourners. The rear of the procession would consist of servants carrying all manner of tomb goods (statuettes, chairs, a bed, boxes of linen, foodstuffs and jewelry), followed by an ox destined for sacrifice at the burial ground, and the colleagues and friends of the deceased.

Illustration 41

Illustration 46

At the tomb courtyard, the coffin would be placed upright while a priest recited incantations from a roll of papyrus. The eldest son of the deceased would also read a number of sacred spells, playing the role of Horus, devoted son to the dead Osiris. The climax of the rites was the ceremony "Opening of the Mouth," through which the mummy would be revitalized and assured of the powers once enjoyed in life. Afterwards, the *ka* statue, and indeed all the images in the tomb, could be similarly revived, so that they could play their particular roles in the afterlife. When the coffin, wreathed with flowers, had been deposited in the burial shaft, the tomb itself was ritually swept clean. The shaft was filled with rubble and sealed with a plaster wall bearing the stamp of the cemetery officials.

With all burial rites completed, the funeral's guests settled down to a banquet feast under a tent. As they ate, they were entertained by singers and harpists who mixed praises of the deceased with songs about the impermanence of human life. An empty chair, cradling a bouquet of flowers, marked the invisible presence of the deceased, so that he too enjoyed the banquet's pleasures.

At length the mourners would drift away, and the last to leave would bury symbolic remnants of the feast, as well as materials left over from the mummification process, a short distance away from the tomb. But the tomb would not be forgotten. For many years funerary priests and family members would continue to come to the open chapel above the burial shaft to offer prayers and gifts of fresh food. But eventually the flow of visitors would cease and only the magic of the spells would remain to provide for the eternal needs of the deceased.

17
SENWOSRET III AS A SPHINX (DETAIL)
Diorite
L., 0.33 m.
Provenance unknown
12th Dynasty, *circa* 1850 B.C.

Since about 3000 B.C. Egyptian society had been divided into clearly defined social classes, the wealthiest being the royal family and below them the nobility. The pharaoh was at the apex of society and enjoyed extraordinary power and prestige, indicated in the Old Kingdom by the large size of the royal pyramids and the unique nature of royal iconography. These traditions were revived in the Twelfth Dynasty, after the country had been reunited under the Eleventh Dynasty. The sphinx representing pharaoh Senwosret III is one of many examples of this revival. Carved in diorite, a rare and expensive stone, it shows Senwosret as a lion with the king's head.

Since the Old Kingdom, the pharaohs' vcitories over Egypt's foreign enemies had been symbolized by such figures, which also recalled the universal and successful struggle of the gods against the forces of general chaos. Sphinxes were therefore appropriate guardians of sacred places; a gigantic one guarded the entrance to the pyramid field of Giza, and in the Middle Kingdom and later sphinxes such as this one stood at the entrances to temples and royal palaces.

(Courtesy of the Metropolitan Museum of Art; gift of Edward S. Harkness, 1916-17; 17.9.2)

18
THE GARDENER, MERER
Diorite
H., 0.28 m.
Buhen, an Egyptian fortress in Lower Nubia
13th Dynasty, *circa* 1780 B.C.

Most Egyptians belonged to the poor class of agricultural laborers, but a slightly better-off middle class emerged in the Middle Kingdom. This sector of Egyptian society was able to afford modest tomb furnishings to decorate their offering chapels. However, at this time, the threat of theft was well recognized, so some of these statuettes, perhaps including that of Merer, were placed in the sealed-off burial chamber itself, to give them extra protection.

(University Museum: E10751)

19

20

19
COFFIN OF DJEHUTY-NAKHT
Wood
L., 2.2 m.
el-Bersheh, where the deceased was a provincial
governor for Senwosret III
12th Dynasty, *circa* 1850 B.C.

The decorated coffins of the First Intermediate
Period (see **14**) became increasingly elaborate during the Middle Kingdom. Here, on the interior face
of the side of the outer wooden coffin of Djehuty-
Nakht, a finely painted false door symbolizes the
deceased's ability to pass from the tomb chamber
to the offering chapel; the mummy lay on its side
with its face towards the door. Right of this door
Djehuty-Nakht, as a *ka*-statue, is shown receiving
offerings. Texts above this scene invoke the aid of
funerary gods and refer to the offerings. At the top
right of the coffin the offerings themselves are listed,
with kneeling men presenting them to the deceased.
Finally, the area at the lower right is filled with
numerous columns of ''Coffin Texts,'' incised in
cursive hieroglyphs and intended to provide the deceased with powerful protective spells for his afterlife.

(Courtesy of the Museum of Fine Arts, Boston:
A2213)

20
THE MUMMY OF WAH
L., 1.67 m.
Thebes
11th Dynasty, *circa* 2000 B.C.

The small tomb of Wah was discovered in late
March 1920 by Herbert E. Winlock, who was then
director of the Egyptian Expedition of the Metropolitan Museum at Thebes. The tomb's entrance lay
hidden among the rubble of a far bigger tomb
opened up a few weeks earlier, that of the nobleman Meket-re',, who served the pharaoh Seankh-
kare' of the Eleventh Dynasty. Wah's coffin and
mummy lay at the rear of the tomb chamber, covered by a pile of laundered bed linen, the mummy
itself being swathed in huge quantities of linen sheet
and bandages almost as fresh as the day they were
buried.

The eventual unwrapping of the mummy, in 1935,

proved to be an intriguing affair. Markings on the bed linen had indicated Wah to be simply an "Overseer of a Storehouse," yet the body was profusely decorated with jewelry from head to toe, at successive levels in the wrappings. There were two large silver scarabs (beetle-shaped stamp seals) placed at Wah's wrists, and these had been oddly mutilated by a methodical hammering and pecking, as if to blind the creature. Many of the inner sheets of linen bore hieroglyphic signs of quality in one corner, and often the owner's name in the opposite corner, indicating Wah worked for Meket-re' for about four years. But many of these owner's labels had been mutilated or torn out, probably at the very time the mummy was being wrapped. So few of the mummies prepared in the Eleventh Dynasty have survived that we are unlikely ever to determine whether any of the features of Wah's treatment were typical of embalming practices at that time or, for some obscure reason, peculiar to Wah himself.

(Courtesy of The Metropolitan Museum of Art, New York; Museum Excavations, 1919-20; Rogers Fund, supplemented by contribution of Edward S. Harkness: 20.3.203)

21

THE MUMMY OF SEKENENRE' II (DETAILS OF THE HEAD AND ARMS)
Deir el-Bahri: the royal cache, found in 1881
17th Dynasty, *circa* 1575 B.C.

During the Twelfth Dynasty, Egypt successfully prevented any recurrence of infiltration by Asiatics from Palestine of the kind which had added to the troubles of the First Intermediate Period. The Thirteenth Dynasty however was weakened by internal Egyptian problems, and groups of urbanized Asiatics (the "Hyksos") succeeded in occupying the eastern Delta. They captured Memphis *circa* 1700 B.C. and were soon recognized as overlords of the entire country. A new Egyptian dynasty developed at Thebes; at first formally subordinate to the Hyksos, it gradually became more independent and eventually began a war of liberation, particularly during the reigns of Kamose and his brother and successor Ahmose. The latter forced the Hyksos out of Egypt altogether and founded the Eighteenth Dynasty.

Seqenenre' II, the father of Kamose, is believed to have died in battle in one of the early military skirmishes against the Hyksos. Study of the skull indicates that the ugly smashes (a-e), judging by their shape, were caused by blows of an axe-head. But a recent x-ray analysis (by the German scientist Erhard Metzel) has shown that the bone around the damage point (a), at least, had partially regrown, so the pharaoh must have sustained this injury some months before his death. It is this earlier incident that is thought to be the cause of the partial paralysis still evident in one of the arms of the mummy. The death-blow was probably a spear-thrust which penetrated the skull behind the left ear.

(*After* G. Elliot Smith, 1912: *Catalogue Général des Antiquitiés Egyptiennes du Musée du Caire*, plates I and II. [L'Institut Francais, Cairo])

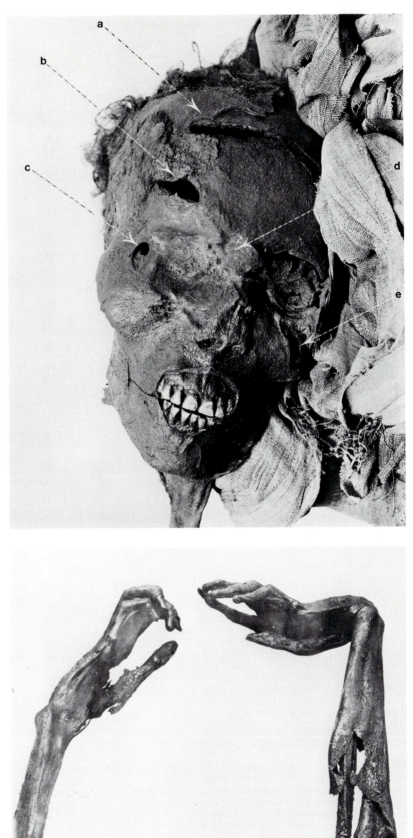

22

SHAWABTI FOR THE SONGSTRESS OF AMUN,
NUBNEFRET
Sandstone
H., 0.28 m.
Aniba, tomb SA 14
circa 1275 B.C.

In ancient Egypt, every citizen was, in principle,
obliged to perform certain kinds of manual labor on
behalf of the national government. Such labor
(called *corvée*) could include the clearance of irri-
gation canals, rebuilding dykes, and general agricultural tasks. The Egyptians believed this labor
would be required of them on behalf of the gods in
the afterlife as well, so they introduced small
figurines, called shawabtis, into the tomb furnishings. The shawabti undertook the tasks of the
corvée on behalf of the deceased.

The tasks themselves were spelled out in an inscription on the shawabti's body, the text corresponding
to all or part, of Chapter 6 of the "Book of the
Dead." The portion of this chapter on the shawabti
of Nubnefret reads, ". . . may the Osiris, the songstress Nubnefret, be illuminated; she says 'O this
shawabti, if the Osiris, the songstress Nubnefret is
summoned and enrolled, to do any work which is to
be done in the cemetery,' (the shawabti will answer)
'I will do it, behold me,' you will say; or if to im-
plant any obstacle there, 'I will do it, behold me'
you will say."

Shawabtis were one of the longest lasting items of
Egyptian funerary equipment; examples of them are
found in burials as late as the Roman era.
(University Museum: E11093)

23

SHAWABTI FOR THE STEWARD MAH
Sandstone
Aniba, tomb SA 14
circa 1275 B.C.

This shawabti is represented dressed in the elaborate pleated garments worn in everyday life by the
nobility of the Nineteenth Dynasty. Instead of the
usual Chapter 6 from the "Book of the Dead," the
shawabti bears quite a different text:

May the Osiris, the deputy Mah, be illuminated:
he says, may your sight be opened, may you
see the sun disc; may you worship Re' in life;
may you be summoned in the cemetery; may
you wander the hills of Tjaumut; may you tra-
verse the mountain of the upper cemetery; may
you behold the hidden cavern; may you sit on
the throne in the sacred land, like the great
crews (of the solar barque of Re'); the steward
Mah.

The artistic quality of this shawabti is extremely
high. Despite the granular nature of sandstone, a
great deal of minute detail was maintained in the
carving.

(University Museum: E11092)

24

STATUE OF AMUNEMHET
Black diorite
H., 0.37 m.
Buhen
circa 1490 B.C.

From the Middle Kingdom on it was customary for wealthy Egyptians to place statues of themselves in temples, in order to display their piety and to ensure that, once deceased, they would share in the daily food and other offerings made by priests to the gods on behalf of the pharaoh. Amunemhet, an official of Hatshepsut (one of the few queens to assume the power of a pharaoh in Egypt) had such a statue placed in the temple of Horus, at Buhen. Although he is depicted as completely Egyptian in physical appearance and in dress, Amunemhet was actually a local Nubian chieftain; through the Egyptianization of such men Egyptian culture, including funerary beliefs and rituals, began to spread into the northern Sudan.

(University Museum: E10980)

25

"THE CELESTIAL WORLD" (DETAIL)
Valley of the Kings; ceiling of the Tomb of Seti I
19th Dynasty, *circa* 1280 B.C.

At the beginning of the New Kingdom the custom of building a separate pyramid for each royal burial was abandoned. The royal tombs were cut into the faces of a deep "Valley of the Kings" in the desert hills of western Thebes, where they could be easily guarded against robbery. The great peak of western Thebes served as a natural pyramid and the funerary temples were built in a row along its eastern foot. The royal tombs and their decoration were modeled on the Egyptian's concept of the royal afterlife. Prepared as long, rock-cut tunnels, they literally represented the underworld with their walls covered with scenes depicting the triumphal progress of the sun-god through this region; by identifying with the sun-god the pharaoh was thought to be guaranteed eternal life. The tunnel ended in the burial chamber, whence the pharaoh's spirit could arise into the sky. The ceilings of these chambers, like that of Seti I, were sometimes covered with yellow figures on a black ground, showing the various constellations of the night sky familiar to the Egyptians, all transformed into gods and legendary beings.

(Courtesy of P. Brodie, University Museum, University of Pennsylvania)

26

A VIEW OF DEIR EL-MEDINEH

Cutting and decorating the royal tomb went on throughout a pharaoh's reign and required skilful and well-trained artisans. They ensured that the walls were cut straight and had smooth surfaces on which they drew figures and texts later carved in relief and painted; in these deep passages lamps filled with oil were used, with salt added to prevent smoke from blackening the walls. Early in the New Kingdom a community of such artisans was established in a village at Deir el-Medineh, to the south of the Valley of the Kings. Generations of these craftsmen lived there and continued to create the royal tombs for over four hundred years. The view illustrated here is of the terraced hillsides on which the villagers built their tombs, many originally topped by the small brick pyramids typical of New Kingdom burial.

(Courtesy of B. Fishman, Oriental Institute, Chicago)

27

THE GODDESS SELKET
Gold
H., 0.89 m.
Valley of the Kings, from the Tomb of Tutankhamun
1325 B.C.

Selket, along with her companions Isis, Nepthys, and Neith, protected the internal organs of the deceased. Her particular responsibility, the intestinal matter, was placed in a miniature coffin; an inscription written in a column down the front attests to her protective nature. She aided the deceased in his journey through the netherworld, and would fight against the evil serpent Apophis. The emblem with which she is associated, the scorpion, rests upon her head, and the power of her magic was great enough to cure its sting. Each of the four goddesses found in Tutankhamun's tomb stood on a side of the canopic chest and faced toward it with outstretched arms. This protective gesture appears to be rather atypical, but only because the statue is removed from its context. Selket, like each of the other goddesses, has a counterpart among the Four Sons of Horus: Kebehsenuef.

(Courtesy of the Metropolitan Museum of Art, New York)

28

KNEELING FIGURE OF TUTANKHAMUN
Bronze, selectively inlaid with gold foil
H., 0.21 m.
Provenance unknown, possibly Memphis
circa 1330 B.C.

Late in the Eighteenth Dynasty, pharaoh Akhenaten caused a major upheaval in Egypt's religious beliefs, by emphasizing the worship of the god Aten (the sun-disc) to the exclusion of almost all other deities. But this change was short-lived, and when Akhenaten died (in 1334 B.C.) his successor Tutankhamun sought to re-establish the power of all the national gods, particularly Amun-Re'. New priests were appointed, old tombs were repaired, and traditional shrine figures were produced in quantity. This statuette was such a figure and was intended to portray the pharaoh in an act of devotion before one of the gods.

(University Museum: E14295)

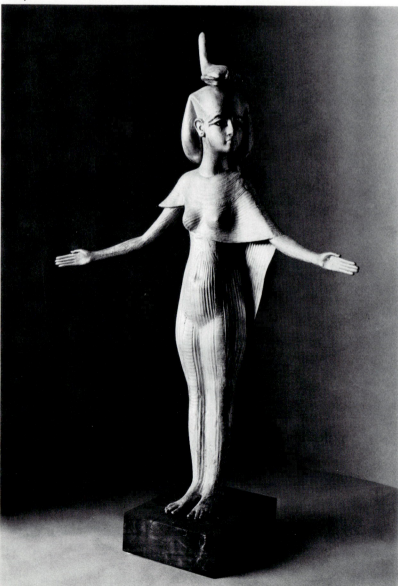

29
PAPYRUS OF ANI (DETAIL)
Thebes
circa 1420 B.C.

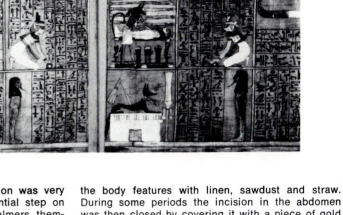

One vignette shows the god of embalming, Anubis, watching over the mummy in the burial chamber. Only three canopic jars lie beside the funeral couch, the customary fourth one probably being excluded by the artist so that he could accommodate Anubis' legs.

The squares immediately surrounding the mummy contain the four Sons of Horus, the goddesses Isis and Nepthys, a *djed*-pillar, and a crouching Anubis. Outer columns of the text are occupied by two *ba*-birds, two flame symbols, and two shawabti figures. Each figure addresses the mummy, offering to protect it.

(Courtesy of the Trustees of the British Museum: 10470)

29-36
THE EMBALMER'S WORKSHOP

For the ancient Egyptians, **mummification was very** much a religious ritual: just one **essential step** on the path to immortality. For the embalmers themselves, however, mummification was a craft requiring deft surgical skills, and, no doubt, quite a strong stomach, for the embalmer's workshop can hardly have been a pleasant place. The daily heat of Egypt meant that decay of a body would set in very soon after death and, in the workshop area itself, the floors probably had to be constantly washed down with water and disinfected with natron.

Traditionally, mummification took seventy days to complete. According to Ptolemaic sources the first half of this period was spent on the initial steps of treating the body. Usually the brain was removed first (see 34), then the left flank was laid open with a flint knife and the entire contents of the abdomen and thorax (with the exception of the heart) were extracted. The viscera were dressed with a scented oil and molten resin before being wrapped in neat linen bundles. (Before the Twentieth Dynasty these bundles were placed in canopic jars—see 36—, but subsequently they were returned to the body cavity —see 66.) Meanwhile, the body cavity had been thoroughly rinsed with palm wine and probably sprinkled with some spices, and the body laid in a bed of natron to drain.

The second half of the mummification period began when the body was removed from the natron and washed free of all residual salts. At this point, the body was little more than a skeleton draped with loose folds of skin: most of the muscle and soft tissues were completely **dissolved or broken** down. So now some time **was spent plumping out** the body features with linen, sawdust and straw. During some periods the incision in the abdomen was then closed by covering it with a piece of gold foil, or a tablet of beeswax impressed with a *wadjet* eye (see **37**) and pouring molten resin over it to keep it in place. The embalmers then smeared the length of the body with a lotion of juniper mixed with beeswax and spices—perhaps cosmetics were applied as well to emphasize facial features such as the eyebrows—and then the wrapping of the mummy began.

This wrapping proceeded with many prayers and rituals. The fingers and toes were sometimes wrapped separately, then each limb, then the head and the torso. Each subsequent wrapping took in greater areas of the body surface, so that the ribbon-like linen strips closest to the body were overlaid by bandages and eventually by sizeable sheets some few meters long. Sawdust was often sprinkled between successive linen layers, and more aromatic oils poured on lightly to impregnate the surface with a heavy scent. Once the body shape had been defined by the tightness of the bandaging, a heavier coat of resin was applied. Jewelry and amulets were then included, before larger shrouds of coarser linen were wound around the entire body, and bound in place by further bandages stretched lengthwise and across it. In all, the amount of cloth used in preparing a mummy could have been equivalent to a strip 300 meters long and varying in width from one centimeter to five meters.

The completed mummy, once garlanded with flowers and laid in a coffin, was ready for the funerary ritual.

30
VESSELS AND MATERIALS FOR AN EMBALMER'S WORKSHOP
H., 0.31 m. (Syrian vessel)
Provenance, various
18th and 19th Dynasties

These materials are typical of the kind that would have been used by an embalmer during the preparation of a body for mummification: a wide-mouthed vessel for straw, another for water or oil, a dish of natron rolled into pellets, a dish for sawdust, a narrow-necked bottle (from Syria) containing an expensive aromatic oil, and the elegant *hes*-flask often depicted in tomb scenes of ritual purification of the body after natron dessication (see below).

(University Museum: E11314, E11312, E11245, **E6996,** and E10433)

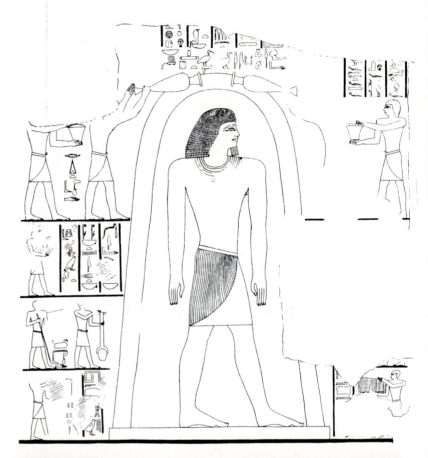

31

PURIFICATION SCENE FROM THE TOMB OF
DJEHUTY-HOTEP
el-Bersheh
12th Dynasty, *circa* 1880 B.C.

After the body was removed from the natron bed it
was ritually washed. Just as the dead pharaoh was
revitalized by this ceremony, reflecting the rejuvena-
tion of Osiris by the waters of the Nile, so should
Djehuty-hotep be revitalized. Two of his sons pour
water from his vessels, while two more sons present
bowls of natron which would have been mixed with
water to improve its cleaning properties. In the
second register, behind Djehuty-hotep, a priest re-
cites a spell, "Unite for you, your bones. What be-
longs to you is complete."

Other versions of this scene show the dead man
crouched over a large pottery vessel which collects
the liquid pouring off the body. The residuals collected in this way would have been thought of as
part of the deceased's 'essence' and so would
have been carefully set aside for disposal in the
embalmer's cache near the tomb (see **46**).

(Scene: *after* P. E. Newberry, 1894: *El-Bersheh* 1,
plate X. Egypt Exploration Fund)

32

X-RADIOGRAPH

In this x-ray, a modern stainless steel probe passes
through the entrance to the nose, through the
cribriform plate of the ethmoid bone (as fractured
by the embalmers) and thus into the cranial cavity.
The pathway to the brain across the skull cavity
was long and narrow, but when an instrument was
inserted in this way and withdrawn, the end (whether
open or coiled) would have held a covering of brain
tissue which was viscous in nature. Repeated in-
sertion of such an instrument would have caused
severe lacerations of the tissue and eventually reduced it to a semi-fluid condition, so that much of
the brain matter could eventually be drained away.

(Courtesy of Dr. F. Filce Leek)

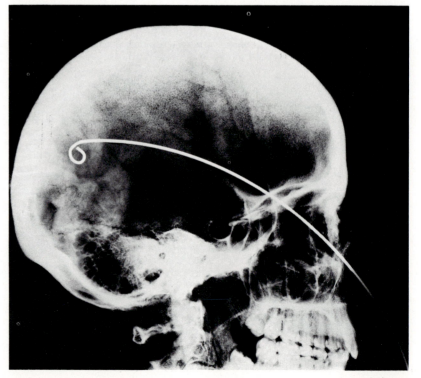

33

THE FOUR SONS OF HORUS
Thebes, from the Tomb of Nebamun and Ipuki
circa 1380 B.C.

The sons of Horus are seated behind Osiris, who holds a flail and crooked staff. These deities were the protectors of the individual organs eviscerated during the first stages of the embalming process. The human-headed Imsety guarded the liver and gall bladder; the ape-headed Hapy, the lungs; the hawk-headed Kebehsenuef, the intestines. The image of the fourth son, Duamutef, is sadly lost in this tomb painting: he guarded the stomach (see **36**).

(Courtesy of the Metropolitan Museum of Art, New York: 30.5.157)

34

CANOPIC JAR
Blue-glazed faience
H., 0.30 m.
Cemetery at Sedment
circa 1250 B.C.

The jackal-headed Duamutef sculpted on the top of this jar was the guardian of the organs of the stomach. The jar itself would have contained these organs after they had been eviscerated during the first stages of the embalming process.

(University Museum: E14227a,b)

35
WADJET EYE AMULETS
Green-glazed and cream-glazed faience
L., 0.050 m. and 0.045 m.
Provenance, unknown and Mit-Rahineh
New Kingdom

The *wadjet eye* was one of the principal amulets used in mummification and might be found among the wrappings in various places on the upper half of the body. (No less than eight were used in the Late Period burial of Djedhor—see 40. The X-ray study of the Ptolemaic mummy Hapi-Men revealed one laid on the deceased's brow—see 105.) It was also the motif impressed upon the wax tablet which covered the incision made by the embalmer when he eviscerated the body.

In texts of the Pyramid era, it was identified with a variety of offerings presented to the deceased pharaoh, particularly with white substances such as milk, natron, linen and frankincense. In the Middle Kingdom it was often painted on the side of the coffin, so that the deceased lying on his left side could look out.

The eye itself was symbolic of the one Seth tore from Horus during their struggle for the throne of Egypt, as described in the Osiris legend (see 5). It was eventually restored to Horus by the ibis-headed god, Thoth. Its role in the funeral ritual was to ensure the revitalization of the deceased and the continuation of good health in the afterlife.

(University Museum: E5079 and 29-85-717)

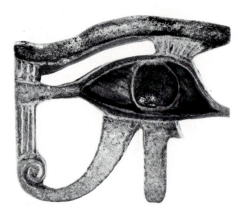

36
MUMMY OF YUYA (DETAIL)
Valley of the Kings
18th Dynasty, *circa* 1350 B.C.

Early in his reign Amunhotep III took as his wife a woman named Tiy, the daughter of Yuya (the pharaoh's Master of Horses) and the lady Thuya. Tiy's parents, although not of royal lineage, did achieve appreciable power and wealth by virtue of their daughter's marriage. The tomb of Yuya and Thuya, the only non-royal one in the Valley of the Kings, was discovered in 1905. It contained fine furnishings despite heavy looting in ancient times.

The mummies of this couple are among the best preserved and the most elegantly prepared examples of the embalmer's craft. Their long reddish-blond hair and carefully restored facial features create a strong lifelike appearance.

(Courtesy of James E. Harris, University of Michigan, Ann Arbor)

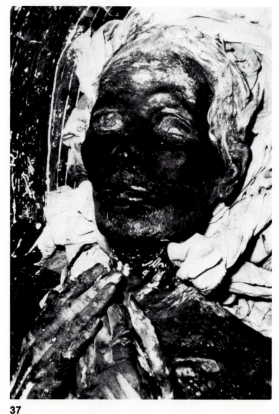

37
SECTION OF THE "BOOK OF THE DEAD" OF NEFER-RENPET
H., 0.36 m.
Deir el-Medineh
circa 1260 B.C.

Nefer-renpet was a sculptor who lived in the village of Deir el-Medineh which housed many of the artisans and craftsmen who were responsible for building and decorating the royal and private tombs of the New Kingdom. Many of these people had their tombs built in the nearby hills, and that of Nefer-renpet is known as Theban Tomb 336. It is likely that he lived some time around 1260 B.C., during the reign of Ramesses II, and that in his later years he was spending appreciable time on the preparation for his final journey. To ensure his success, he had a Book of the Dead prepared, to be put into his tomb when he died. For extra protection, he had another book, now in Brussels, put in his tomb

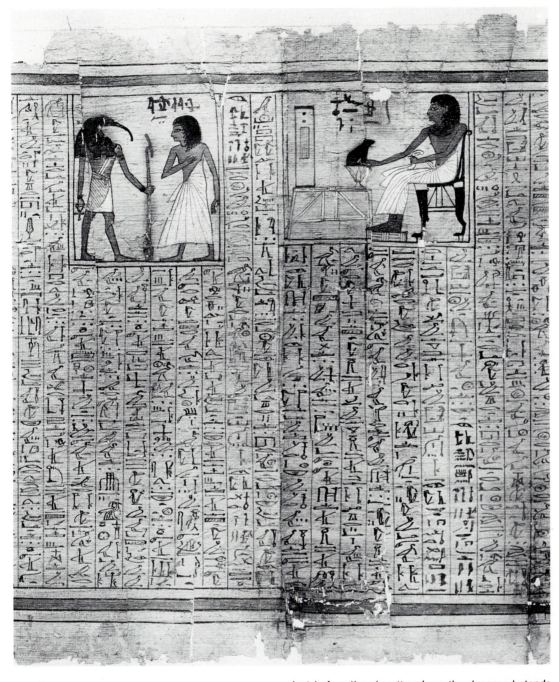

as well.

Many of these collections of spells were prepared in advance by the artist/scribe who would personalize them by inscribing the name of the owner in the appropriate spots in the text and near the figure of the deceased in the vignettes. No one papyrus contains all of the known spells which number almost two hundred. Each papyrus contains several spells, and the section here has Spells 94, 96, 97 and part of 130.

Spell 94, for requesting a water jar and palette in the cemetery, begins just under the front leg of the chair upon which Nefer-renpet sits. Upon the table is some of the scribal equipment for which he asks. Nefer-renpet emphasizes his virtues and identifies with the activities of the scribe of the gods, Thoth, and he ends the text with a promise: "I will act righteously so that I might go righteously to Re' and to Osiris the course of everyday."

Just before the vignette where the deceased stands opposite Thoth, Spell 96, with its continuation 97, begins: "A spell for being beside Thoth and causing a man to attain a blessed state in the cemetery." The following lines have the deceased reciting the deeds he has done in appeasing some gods and expressing statements of his righteous behavior.

The columns to the right form the terminal section of Spell 130 which is to be uttered over the bark of Re'. The text explains one of the "mysteries" of the netherworld and affirms that the deceased, who is judged to be righteous, identifies with Re'. It is stated that the *ba* will live forever and that it will not again be in the cemetery. To ensure his survival, the end of the spell reads: "His offerings will be upon the altar of Re' in the course of everyday, and he will be in an excellent state of blessedness in the cemetery . . ."

(University Museum: E2775)

38

AMULET IN THE SHAPE OF A PAPYRUS STALK
Green feldspar
H., 0.068 m.
Ramesseum (the mortuary temple of Ramesses II)
New Kingdom

The details are finely carved, and traces of its original gold leaf still exist at the base and close to the top. In sunken relief around the shaft of the amulet are six columns of hieroglyphs that comprise one of the very short spells of the "Book of the Dead," Chapter 159. The title, which was omitted ostensibly for lack of space, is "A spell for the papyrus of feldspar to be put at the throat of the blessed one." The amulet refers to the deceased as "the Osiris, the chief of the gold workers [of Amun], Amunhotep," and it was fashioned for him and was to be put upon the neck of his mummy. Although not inscribed on this item, the next chapter of the "Book of the Dead" also concerns the papyrus amulet and indicates its importance for the deceased: "If it stays sound, I stay sound; if it stays uninjured, I stay uninjured . . ."

Small finds such as this amulet were discovered in the late New Kingdom burials at the Ramesseum, and can date as early as the Eighteenth Dynasty. Most of this material, however, dates to the Twenty-second Dynasty.

(University Museum: E13413)

39

HEART SCARAB
Green schist
L., 0.13 m.
Aniba (in Nubia)
New Kingdom

This piece is referred to as a heart scarab because it has inscribed on its underside a version of Chapter 30 B of the "Book of the Dead," which is devoted to the protection of the heart during the judgment of the deceased. Some heart scarabs begin with an invocation to prepare the scarab and to put it within the chest of the deceased. The inscription here omits this opening, but instead implores: "My heart of my mother, my breast, (my) being! Stand not against me as witness in (?) the council. Do not tilt against me before the keeper of the balance. You are my *ka* which is in my body . . ." The remainder of the inscription tells the heart to aid in presenting the deceased at the time of judgment as one worthy to enter the afterlife. The name of the deceased Pahory (who the excavator assumed was a Nubian) is written on the top, across the wings, as well as on the back, though it is spelled in two different ways.

Heart scarabs were regularly included among the necessities of the deceased. Should any damage come to the heart itself, the scarab could serve as its substitute. It has been suggested that they could replace the real heart in the final judgment to ensure entrance to the afterlife.

(University Museum: E11013)

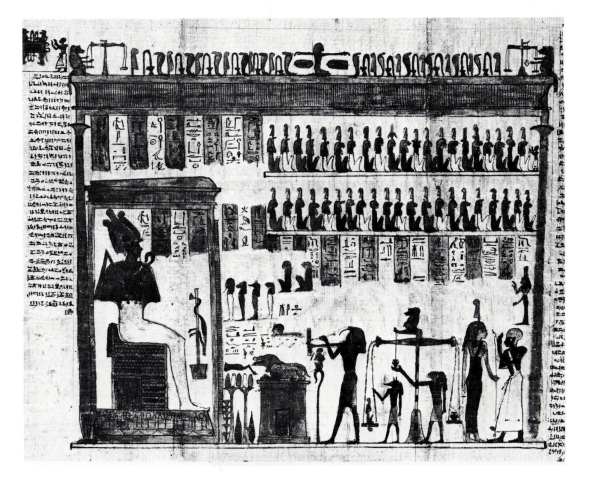

40
PAPYRUS RYERSON (DETAIL): "THE JUDGMENT
OF THE DEAD"
H., 0.38 m.
Provenance unknown
Persian-Ptolemaic period

Though quite late in date, the format of this papyrus is typical of that used to portray the judgment scene from the New Kingdom onwards.

The deceased is represented here by his heart, which symbolizes his existence on earth. It is being weighed in the scale, and it must balance against the goddess Maat (seated in the other pan) who represents justice, harmony and order. Thoth, scribe of the gods, stands before the scale recording the verdict, and Osiris, lord of the underworld, is enthroned beneath the canopy and oversees the action. Should the heart of the deceased not balance with Maat, a creature (here seated on a shrine) that is part lion, part hippopotamus and part crocodile will devour it. Assorted minor deities are present as well. The inscription, which reads from the right to the left at first and then alternates, is part of Chapter 125 of the "Book of the Dead," a collection of spells used by the deceased as an aid in entering the afterlife: "Words said by Osiris: 'Maat, Mistress of the West, may she cause his name to be in his temple united (with) his cavern of eternity.' The Foremost of the Divine Booth, he says: 'The heart is precise; the balance is filled with the Osiris [Name omitted], justified son of [Name

omitted] justified, living forever and ever.' Words said by the Lord of Heliopolis, Lord of Divine Words (hieroglyphs): 'Put his heart in its place for him, for the Osiris justified.' "

Over the four figures directly in front of the booth of Osiris are the names: "Imseti, Hapy, Duamutef, and Kebehsenuef." They are the four sons of Horus, the protectors of the viscera of the deceased. Two further figures seated behind them are identified as "Fate and Fortune." In front of the creature on the shrine is the inscription: "Subduing of enemies by the she-gobbler of the West in the West." Behind the four sons of Horus is a designation of another deity Meskhenet, a birth-goddess.

Before Osiris, from right to left, are a designation and a series of epithets for the deity: "Osiris, Wennefer, Lord of Abydos, Foremost of the West, Ruler of Eternity, Lord of Life, Great One, Lord of Eternity." Above his shrine with the same orientation are more of the same: "Osiris, Wennefer, Lord of Life, Great God, Ruler of Eternity, Chief of the Necropolis, and the Place of Silence, Foremost of the West, Great God, Lord of Abydos, King of Eternity, Ruler of the living, of gods and of mankind, Great One [in] heaven and earth, Sovereign."

(Courtesy of the Oriental Institute, University of Chicago: 9787)

41

THE FUNERAL OF RAMOSE
Thebes, from the Tomb of Ramose, vizier to the
Pharaoh Amunhotep III and, briefly, to the Pharaoh
Akhenaten.
circa 1340 B.C.

Burial rituals were depicted in tomb chapels as
early as the Old Kingdom, but the most detailed
examples, such as that of the funeral of Ramose
illustrated in a line drawing here, date to the New
Kingdom.

On the left the funerary procession approaches the
tomb. In the rear are Ramose's subordinates, the
chief government officials of the period. Before
them, in the upper register, we see (from left to
right) a shrine containing the canopic jars, a larger
one with the coffin inside it and a crouching man
wrapped in an animal skin. Each of these is on a
sled pulled by men; the cattle in front of the procession had hauled the sleds until the ground,
closer to the tomb, became too uneven. Since the
deceased is equated with Osiris, women representing Osiris' wife Isis and his sister Nepthys ac-
company the coffin.

The remainder of the procession, in the lower register, consists of two groups of servants—one on the
right carrying food and floral offerings, another on
the left carrying furniture, wine jars and other items
—and women from Ramose's household. The women
turn to face the coffin, throwing dust on their heads
and weeping, as signs of mourning. On the right
Hathor, patron goddess of the Theban cemetery
where Ramose was buried, witnesses the final rites
at the tomb. Below, the "Opening of the Mouth"
ritual (sadly very poorly preserved here, but see **42**)
is performed on the mummies of Ramose and his
wife; above, food offerings are carried toward the
stela, carved as a false door, in the tomb chapel.

(*After* N. de Garis Davies, 1941: *Mond Excavations
at Thebes 1,* plates XXIII-XXVII. The Egyptian Exploration Society, London)

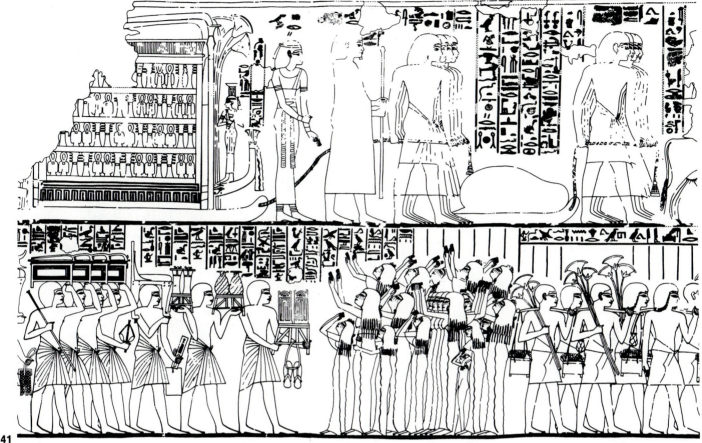

Continued overleaf

41

42
PART OF THE CLIFFS OF WESTERN THEBES
Tombs such as that of Ramose were cut into these cliffs.

(Egyptian Section, University Museum)

42

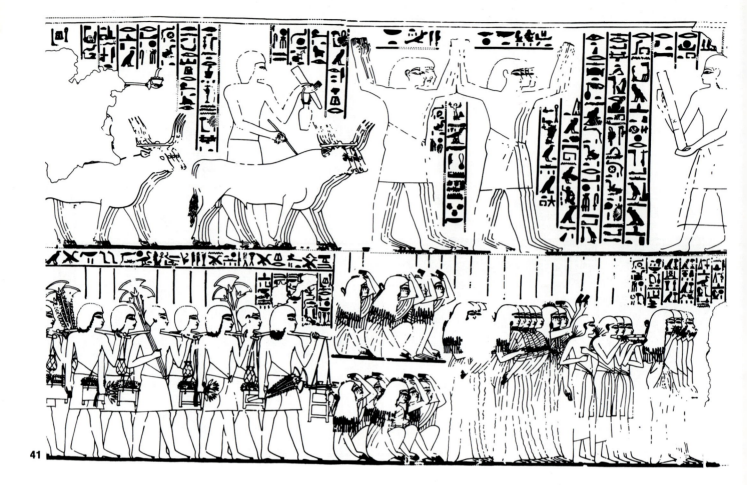

41

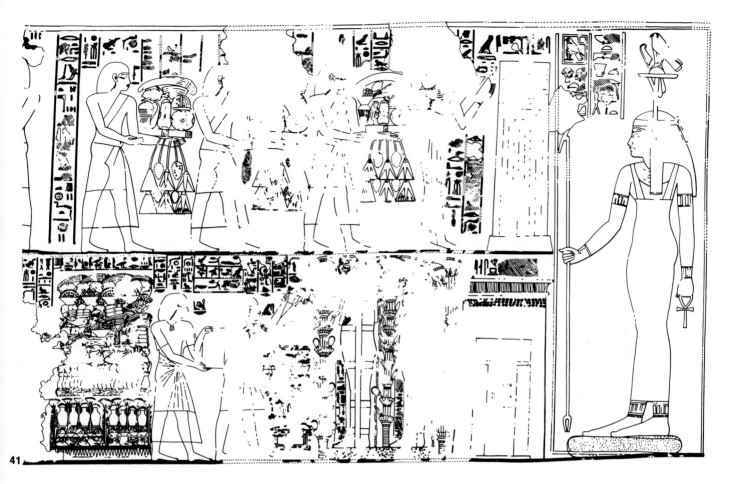

41

43
SHAWABTI BOX, TOGETHER WITH THREE
SHAWABTIS, MADE FOR THE SINGER OF AMUN,
MERY-AMUN-DUA
Wood
H., 0.34 m.
Provenance unknown, probably western Thebes
circa 1200 B.C.

The shrine-like form of this shawabti box is typical
of the New Kingdom when the number of shawabtis
allotted to a burial was relatively small. In later
times, when as many as four hundred shawabtis
might be included in the tomb furnishings, the
shawabtis were stacked horizontally in a much
simpler storage chest.

(University Museum: L-55-23 a-c, and L-55-18, -19,
-20 and -22)

44
"OPENING OF THE MOUTH" CEREMONY
Thebes: scene from the Tomb chapel of Nakhtamun,
an official in the funerary temple of Ramesses II
19th Dynasty, *circa* 1210 B.C.

This ceremony ensured that the mummy would be
able to function in the afterlife (i.e., be able to see,
speak and move, and be able to eat the food offerings piled up in the tomb) and was consequently a
vital part of the funerary ritual. Here the mummy of
Nakhtamun stands upright in front of the tomb, with
a mourning woman kneeling at its feet, and three
priests beside her performing the ceremony itself.
The mummy is purified with natron and water, while
its eyes and its mouth are touched with a model of
a carpenter's adze. An adze was used because the
ritual was originally applied to wooden statues, and
it was this tool which was the principal one used in
manufacturing such figures.

(*After* N. de Garis Davies, 1948: *Seven Private
Tombs at Kurnah,* plate XXVI. The Egypt Exploration
Society, London)

43

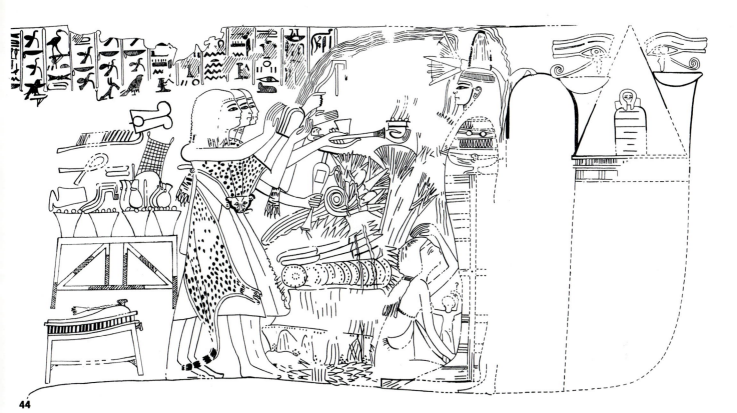

44

45
"THE BANQUET"
Thebes; scene from the Tomb chapel of Nakht,
Scribe and Astronomer of Amun
18th Dynasty, *circa* 1420 B.C.

Such scenes show the living and the dead members
of a family intermingled at a banquet of a type
common in the New Kingdom. In the lower right
the funeral tone is established by the making of
offerings to the tomb owner and his wife. In the
lower left are musicians, and behind them guests
wearing scented cones on their heads. Above, more
guests are entertained by a blind harpist who probably sang of the deceased's virtues and of the
dangers of the underworld.

(*After* N. de Garis Davies, 1917: *Tomb of Nakht at
Thebes,* plate 15. Metropolitan Museum of Art; Robb
de Peyster Tytus Memorial Series, vol. 1.)

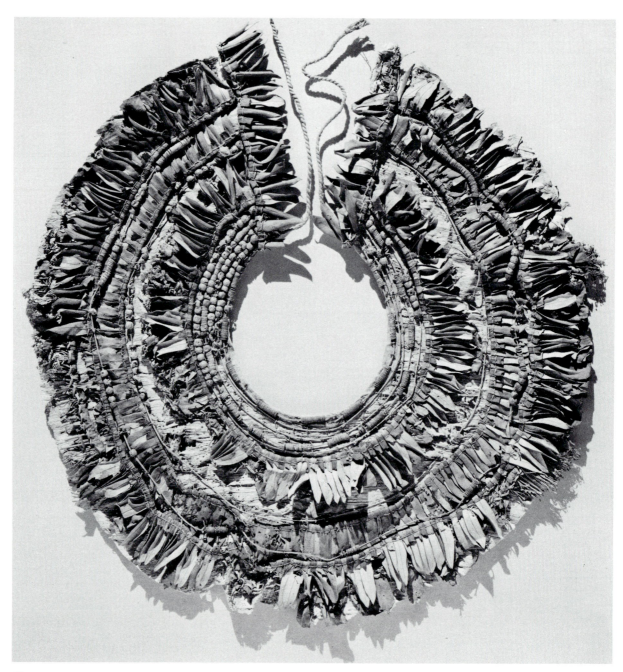

46
FLORAL COLLAR
Papyrus and flowers
H., 0.50 m.
Valley of the Kings; from the embalmers' cache of
Tutankhamun
18th Dynasty, *circa* 1325 B.C.

As the final step in an ancient Egyptian funeral, the pots containing the waste embalming materials, and the remnants of the funeral banquet were gathered up and buried in a pit a short distance away. So it was with the funeral of Tutankhamun when that youthful pharaoh was buried in the Valley of the Kings.

It was early in January 1908 that Theodore M. Davis stumbled upon the cache of waste from Tutankhamun's funeral. The jars were mainly filled with innumerable scraps of linen (probably floor sweepings collected after the body of the pharaoh had been wrapped during mummification), several bags of natron and chopped straw. There were also three fine linen kerchiefs which, in life, would have been worn over a short wig of the kind that was fashionable in Thebes in the Eighteenth Dynasty; and a miniature plaster mask of uncertain significance in the embalming ritual.

Other jars were packed with bones of a cow, of geese and of ducks—the left-overs from the final meal—together with the remains of several collars worn by the banquet guests. Such collars were ingeniously prepared with sheets of papyrus sewn together as backing for concentric rows of olive leaves, cornflowers and the berries of woody nightshade. Even the two brooms used to remove the last footprints made by the guests as they left the banquet were squeezed into the jars, not taken away for further use.

(Courtesy of the Metropolitan Museum of Art, Gift of Theodore M. Davis, 1909: 09.184.216)

V. SPLENDOR, THEN DECLINE

THE RAMESSIDE PERIOD
(1293-1070 B.C.)

The death of Akhenaten in 1334 B.C. ushered in a period of confusion in the country's political structure. Neither of Akhenaten's two successors, Smenkhkare' and Tutankhamun, left an heir; Aye, who had officiated at Tutankhamun's funeral, succeeded him but reigned only briefly, and also produced no heir. The general Horemheb, who had served under Tutankhamun, took control at Aye's death.

Horemheb's long reign of close to twenty-eight years was marked by a completion of the restoration of internal order begun under Tutankhamun, and the reassertion of Egypt's power abroad. He left his prosperous kingdom to his chief official,

Ramesses, the founder of the Nineteenth Dynasty (1293-1185 B.C.). This dynasty was one of the most powerful ever to govern Egypt; it provided its population with a high standard of living. New construction was particularly pronounced, with the reign of Ramesses II being commemorated

Text Figure 13
HYPOSTYLE HALL OF THE TEMPLE OF
AMUN-RE'
Karnak
Early 19th Dynasty, *circa* 1290 B.C.

One of the principal building ventures of Ramesses II, extending an earlier construction by his father, Seti I.

After G. Perrot and C. Chipiez, 1883: *A History of Art in Ancient Egypt*, 368. (Chapman and Hall, London.)

by more buildings than that of any other pharaoh. His achievements include most of the Hypostyle hall at Karnak (begun by his father, Seti I), the massive rock-cut temple at Abu Simbel, and the Ramesseum.

Within this atmosphere of affluence, however, we can identify a number of factors that were beginning to fracture Egyptian national confidence. No longer was Egypt militarily predominant against surrounding lands, and it had to treat as equals the once despised foes, the Hittites of Asia Minor. Sea raiders repeatedly threatened the northern coastline; Libyan forces began to penetrate the western defences. Appropriately, the scenes in private tombs reflect an increased emphasis on religion and rarely depict the once common glimpses of daily life. Religious hymns, as a rule, are still hymns of praise, but an acknowledgment of heavy personal sin is sometimes included. Intense pleas for mercy are now made to the gods.

The Nineteenth Dynasty ended with the various descendants of Ramesses II struggling destructively for pharaonic power. The opportunities provided by this squabbling were seized upon by Setnakht (a man of unknown lineage) to begin the Twentieth Dynasty in 1185 B.C. His son, Ramesses III, managed to preserve the independence of Egypt by defeating three waves of foreign invaders. But his courtiers conspired to assassinate him, and his weak successors were scarcely able to maintain the economic and physical integrity of the kingdom. The Twentieth Dynasty ended, in 1070 B.C., in civil war.

The ebb and flow of events in the Nineteenth and Twentieth Dynasties had little effect upon the craft of mummification. It continued to show increased technical re-

THE FIELDS OF THE BLESSED: A WALL PAINTING FROM THE TOMB OF SENNEDJEM
Deir el-Medineh
circa 1300 B.C.

Sennedjem and his wife work on their estate in the world they entered after death. The land is irrigated by canals—the blue herring-boned strip in the scene—and the couple plow, sow and harvest a fine crop of wheat and flax. In the orchards, the date palms are laden with fruit, while the garden is lush with flowers.

Everything in this scene concentrates on one of several co-existing ideas about the nature of the afterlife. Here death is approached with no particular dread, and with confidence that the afterlife held in store all the best of an Egyptian's normal daily routine. Elsewhere, often in the same tomb, the afterlife would also appear as a place of danger.

(Courtesy of the Metropolitan Museum of Art, New York: 30.4.2)

finement and even novelty. For example, the mummy of Ramesses III provides the first known use of artificial eyes, a change which became standard practice thereafter. A number of substitutes for the usual linen packing of the body cavity can now be documented, including the use of lichens for Siptah and Ramesses IV, and of sawdust laced with aromatics for Ramesses V.

Additionally, the practice of putting viscera in canopic jars became far less common. The individual organs were now bundled in linen, and put back into the body, sometimes with wax models of their guardians, the Four Sons of Horus. This was how Ramesses III was prepared for burial. However, dummy jars continued to be included among the tomb furniture.

The civil strife of the late Twentieth Dynasty did allow tomb robbing to occur on such a wide scale that even the mummies of royalty were stripped of their wrappings and left naked in their vandalized tombs or, in some cases, burned.

Some of the tomb robbers were the unpaid Libyan soldiers who are known to have roamed throughout the Valley of the Kings, striking terror into the local population. Others were the craftsmen who were constructing the tombs and the cemetery guards themselves. Documents detailing the trials of these tomb robbers have survived, and the testimony of one thief provides this description of his attack on a royal tomb of the Seventeenth Dynasty:

". . . We went to rob in the tombs as (was) our regular custom . . . and we found the pyramid of the king Sekhemre Shedtawy . . . son of Sobekemsaf, it not being like the pyramids and tombs of the nobles in which we regularly went to rob . . ., and we found the god (*i.e.* the pharaoh) lying at the rear of his burial place . . ., his queen at his side . . ., and we opened their outer coffins and their inner coffins . . ., and we found the noble body (*sah*) of the king equipped with a sword, and a great number of amulets and jewels of gold being at his neck . . . The noble body of this king was entirely covered with gold, inside and outside . . ." (*Papyrus Leopold-Amherst*).

He and his companions then stripped off the gold, and, in this instance, burnt the bodies.

Such thieves received harsh punishment, but the authorities were unable to prevent the continued desecration of the ancient dead. Some royal mummies were attacked repeatedly, occasionally with extremely destructive results. The mummy of Ramesses

Illustration 66

Illustration 48

VI was literally chopped to pieces by the robbers who used axes to cut through the wrappings and expose the valuables on the body.

In a final attempt to shield the despoiled bodies from further danger, the officials of the Valley of the Kings began to move the mummies from one tomb to another in search of a location isolated enough to provide adequate protection. As the Twentieth Dynasty drew to a close, increasing numbers of both royal and private tombs were left empty, stripped of their funeral goods and often of their deceased owner as well.

REPAIRING THE DAMAGE

The last pharaoh of the New Kingdom was Ramesses XI (1098-1070 B.C.) who, despite a lengthy reign, was unable to prevent a progressive weakening of the country's political structure. Even before his death effective power had passed into other hands. In the north, a nobleman, Smendes, controlled the Delta from his port city of Tanis; in the south, the general, Herihor, governed Upper Egypt from Thebes. With Ramesses XI dead, Smendes formally assumed the throne, but Herihor's descendants remained unchallenged at Thebes. There they also controlled the important position of High Priest of Amun. With these events, the Third Intermediate Period (1070-656 B.C.) opens.

Illustration 62

Illustration 53

Initially there was none of the civil strife which had been a feature of the two earlier Intermediate Periods. The illusion of national unity was maintained by official marriages between members of the Tanite royal family and representatives of the Theban priestly line. Thus Herihor's grandson, the High Priest Pinudjem I, married the Tanite princess, Henettawy. Nevertheless the effective political division of the land made the undertaking of any large-scale building projects and of major military expeditions quite impossible. Nothing characterizes the period better than the temple complexes at Tanis. Outwardly impressive, they prove to have been constructed largely from blocks removed from the monuments of earlier pharaohs.

Illustration 56

In the south the Theban priests busied themselves with the restoration of the battered royal mummies. Eventually two sites were selected: one the cliff-tomb of an Eighteenth Dynasty queen, Inhapi, at Deir el-Bahri, the other the tomb of Amunhotep II in the Valley of the Kings. There, the rewrapped bodies could be safely concealed, along with those of a number of the High Priests themselves and their families. It had not been possible to repair all the damage inflicted by the tomb robbers, given the reduced resources of the Thebans at this time and the poor condition of some of the bodies themselves. Indeed, with Ramesses VI no restoration could be effective, so that his new wrappings were carefully applied over a jumble of fragments, including limbs from other bodies and even bones from food offerings.

There was no question of recreating the glittering wealth once buried with these pharaohs: they were provided with the remnants of their original equipment or with a handful of shoddy substitutes. Even the coffins had to be remade or simply "borrowed" from elsewhere. The only labels on the mummies were the scribal notes, hurriedly written (in the cursive script, hieratic) on the bandages or on the coffin lids, and in a few instances the identity of the body was lost. But when the work was finally complete, the dead were to have almost three thousand years without further disturbance. The priests had performed their task well, and it was not until the nineteenth century A.D. that the hiding places were again discovered.

The embalmers in this late period developed a new technique to minimize the visual effect of shrinkage caused by mummification: they put packing material beneath the skin in order to fill out the bodily features in a realistic way. Special incisions were made with pointed sticks just to the surface of the muscular tissue, so that linen or mud could be inserted beneath the skin alone. Then false eyes of stone and heavy wigs were used to achieve a surprisingly lifelike effect.

Unfortunately the work of the embalmers at Tanis cannot properly be compared with the impressive results obtained by their Theban counterparts. The humid climate of the Delta has reduced the few mummies found there almost to a skeletal state. It would seem that the Tanite pharaohs themselves realized the dangers posed by the northern climate, since their burial equipment was designed to minimize the use of wood and other perishable materials.

DECLINING STANDARDS

The Twenty-second Dynasty, beginning in 945 B.C., only briefly restored the political unity of Egypt. Under its first pharaoh, Sheshonk I, Egyptian armies once more marched against foreign lands, and great buildings once again rose in Thebes. But this national resurgence was short-lived. Within a century a vicious civil war broke out, disrupting the country for some three

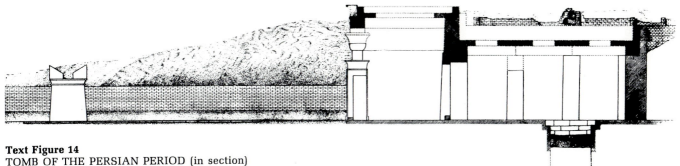

Text Figure 14
TOMB OF THE PERSIAN PERIOD (in section)
Saqqara
circa 500 B.C.

At the rear of a forecourt, a temple-like offering chapel stands above the burial shaft. The shafts of such tombs were often extraordinarily deep and sand-filled, to discourage robbery.
After M. G. Lefebvre, 1923: *Le Tombe de Petosiris*, plate III (L'Institut Français, Cairo.)

decades. There were soon two, then three, and finally four dynastic families controlling different parts of Egypt.

For a brief time Nubian kings reigned as the Twenty-fifth Dynasty, beginning in 728 B.C., but they were expelled by an invasion of Assyrians who sacked Thebes in 663 B.C. and carried off vast quantities of temple wealth. The Assyrians, in their turn, were forced out of the Nile Valley; and, in 656 B.C., one of the local princes, Psammetichus, assumed the throne as the first pharaoh of the Twenty-sixth Dynasty. He restored the internal security of the country, and thereby ended the Third Intermediate Period.

Sadly the burial customs of this phase of Egyptian history reflect the poverty and instability then current. No new techniques of mummification were developed, though a great deal of minor variation is in evidence. For example, the wrapped internal organs are now often placed outside the mummy, without any particular convention for location. The specialized techniques of the Twenty-first Dynasty—particularly that of subcutaneous packing—are scarcely ever used again.

In the tomb itself, the Third Intermediate Period is characterized by the nearly complete disappearance of furnishings in the burials even of the wealthy. The coffins themselves are now the only major item included, as well as dummy canopic jars and boxes of funerary statuettes. This development was almost certainly a consequence of the sheer persistence of tomb robbing: even jewelry tended to be of wood and faience, since it was so unlikely that gold or silver items would stay very long with the deceased.

TOWARDS MASS PRODUCTION

The years of the Twenty-sixth Dynasty (656-525 B.C.) were the last major period of national revival in ancient Egypt. It was a time of confidence and renewal, when the deep roots of native culture were tapped again for fresh inspiration. For example, sculpture was directly modeled upon that of the distant Old, Middle and even New Kingdoms, and attempts were made to restore the great pyramids at Giza.

Funeral practices too were revitalized. Though burial goods remain sparse by New Kingdom standards, such equipment as was produced was made with a renewed concern for craftsmanship. Imposing tombs of stone or brick, together with coffins of the highest quality, appeared once more in the wealthier burials. Meanwhile, the democratization of burial preparation, aided by the introduction of a much less expensive way of extracting the internal organs, had *Illustration 67* advanced a great deal. A turpentine-like substance was introduced anally, and forced into the body cavity, so that the organs were simply reduced to a solution.

Meanwhile the "Book of the Dead" received its final and most thorough revision (so that its collection and order of spells became far more uniform), and amulets *Illustration 70* became yet more diverse in form. But the renewed emphasis on magic was not now a sign of doubt and uncertainty; rather it was just another expression of the willingness of the Twenty-sixth Dynasty to draw on all available symbols of traditional culture, *Illustration 64* and adapt them to current needs.

This exciting resurgence of Egyptian vitality was, however, short-lived. Soon the Persian forces of Cambyses swept into

Egypt (taking Memphis in 525 B.C.), and, although the Egyptians enjoyed another brief period of independence during the Twenty-eighth—Thirtieth Dynasties (404-343 B.C.), the constant pressures from the Persian Empire eventually proved too great. After the Persians, came the Greeks who, under the leadership of Alexander the Great, completed the conquest of Egypt in 332 B.C.; then the Romans seized Egypt, after the Battle of Actium in 31 B.C.

Illustration 68

Illustration 75

The embalmer's skills continued to decline. An increasingly elaborate pattern of wrapping the mummy, together with the lavish use of brightly colored cartonnage masks and breast covers obscured the fact that the preparation of the corpse itself was becoming quite casual. It is particularly noticeable that the body was often allowed to reach a state of quite advanced decay before the embalmers began work at all.

From about the third century B.C. onwards, mummification was so routine that embalming guilds were formed in every sizeable community, and competition between them kept the price of treatment down quite significantly. The practice of dissolving the body organs rather than extracting them became more common; and

Illustration 69

now the brain was often removed through the opening at the base of the skull where it joins the spinal column.

In time, the influence of Greek and Roman culture penetrated deeply into Egyptian funerary practices. Few Egyptians could now understand the ancient spells (and repeated copying increased confusion about their meaning), so that they gradually disappeared from the decoration of the mummy and its coffin. When scenes of funerary significance do survive, they are usually distorted versions of the Osiris legend, and where the name of the deceased was included, it was as often in Greek as in Egyptian. The coffins themselves were gradually replaced by pseudo-coffins of linen or plaster, either topped with a massive gilded headpiece or a portrait of the deceased painted on a wooden panel placed over the face. Some of these portraits are certainly attractive, but have to be recognized as purely Roman in style.

As late as the fourth century A.D. mummies were still being made, but by this time Christianity had been adopted by the majority of the native population. In this faith, body preservation was not required for attaining eternal life, so the practices of extracting internal organs and bandaging the body were set aside. A man would be buried in the clothes he had worn in life.

The fervent leaders of the Christian faith regarded the embalmer's craft as a pagan ritual, and actively purged it from Egyptian society. By the early fifth century A.D., mummies were prepared no more, and a remarkable element of Egyptian cultural heritage was erased after a history of more than three thousand years.

VI. MUMMIFICATION OF ANIMALS

INTRODUCTION

We cannot leave the history of embalming without mention of the practice that entered the funeral ritual of ancient Egypt around the middle of the first millennium B.C.: the mummification of animals. Certainly animals were occasionally afforded the same burial rites as humans in the Badarian period (*circa* 4500 B.C.), but such practices died out soon after, leaving no trace of their inspiration. A variety of animals were regarded as manifestations of gods throughout pharaonic times. Particularly important were the major cults of living bulls—the Mnevis bull at Heliopolis, the Buchis bull at Armant and the Apis bull at Memphis—which stood alone in terms of the level of national worship accorded them throughout their lives, and the elaborate mummification they received in death. However, although pets were occasionally mummified and buried, the systematic mummification of animals began with the Apis bull only in the New Kingdom, and spread to a number of other animals some while later.

The Greek historian Herodotus, who visited Egypt in the fifth century B.C., noted the widespread occurrence of animal worship there. He refrained, however, from commenting negatively about it, filled as he was with respect for the achievements of a civilization far older than his own. But, by the end of the fourth century B.C., many educated Greeks such as Timocles expressed revulsion at this practice. They could not understand that the Egyptians believed the attributes of the gods were given concrete form in certain animals. So the sky-god Horus became a hawk soaring over the concerns of mankind; the fiery goddess Sakhmet, who ruled the affairs of war and plague, was pictured as a lioness.

With other gods the basis for a link to an animal form is now lost to us but probably lies in the predynastic era. At that time, certain animals may have been recognized as emblems for regional population groups, and, by extension, as the principal gods for such groups. After the unification of Egypt some regional gods assumed national importance and began to absorb the identities and appearances of lesser gods with similar religious functions. Thus Thoth, the god of wisdom, could be represented as an ibis or sometimes as a baboon.

ORIGINS

We can reasonably discount any notion that, by mummification, an attempt was being made to carry the animal gods into the afterworld along with the deceased, as some kind of divine retinue. (Some instances of mummification of the dog, sacred to Anubis, may have been exceptions to this generalization.) Otherwise, we would have expected the animal mummies to form part of the tomb equipment of each human burial and such is not the case.

Illustration 85

It is possible that mummified animals were relatively inexpensive alternatives to the carved stone or bronze figures of animal gods which, at this late stage in Egyptian history, were very much in vogue as votive offerings made by the wealthy at their local temples. The near simultaneous growth in popularity of this type of temple furnishing and the practice of animal mummification, seem too coincidental.

At Bubastis, the cat cult in honor of the goddess Bastet, grew to huge proportions, the creatures being commercially bred and slaughtered at the onset of maturity (by breaking their necks), then mummified and offered for purchase by pious pilgrims, (The priest of each shrine then received

Illustration 80

Illustration 82

these tokens of devotion back and entombed them on the pilgrim's behalf.) At Saqqara and Hermopolis, ibis mummies filled the catacombs; at Latopolis (in Upper Egypt) the large Nile fish (*latus*) were so treated. Herodotus has left us a report of the now lost labyrinth of Crocodilopis in the Fayum, where the reptiles, with bejewelled feet, were force-fed on cakes and honeyed drinks in honor of the god Sobek. (On occasion, even the eggs of these crocodiles were mummified individually.) The hawk, as the symbol of Horus, would certainly have been more extensively represented in this pantheon of animal mummies but for its elusiveness to capture. As it was, the lowly shrew, the snake and even the scorpion, each found itself the object of some religious devotion.

The decline of animal mummification (as with that of humans) came with the rapid growth of Christianity in the third century A.D. Eventually only the bull cults remained. The last known hieroglyphic inscription (dating A.D. 295) records the death of the last Buchis bull, and as late as A.D. 362, the Roman emperor Julian, in an attempt to revive pagan rituals in Egypt, instituted a search for a new Apis; he subsequently featured the animal on his coinage. The persistence of Apis worship had frustrated the early Christian militants, but the great bull mausoleum (The Serapeum) at Saqqara was finally destroyed in about A.D. 398 following the edicts of the emperor Honorius banning the maintenance of sanctuaries for pagan use. The passing of Apis ceremonials marked the end of the last significant expression of ancient Egyptian religious belief.

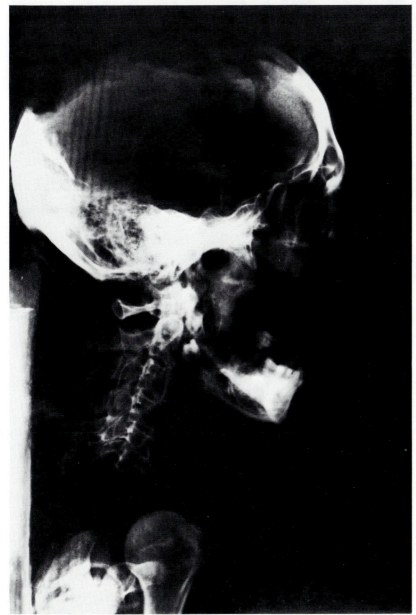

47
RELIEF OF RAMESSES III SMITING HIS ENEMIES
Thebes, on the northern wing of the pylon of the pharaoh's funerary temple
20th Dynasty, *circa* 1160 B.C.

Like his predecessors, Ramesses III was often depicted as a victorious warrior with superhuman capabilities. Here we see him grasping a group of foreign enemies by their hair and raising a combined mace and axe with which he will slaughter them. On the right Amun-Re', the imperial god of the New Kingdom, extends a sword of Asiatic type to the pharaoh and proclaims that he has made all Egypt's enemies powerless before Ramesses. Below are two rows of figures, each representing a city-wall oval containing the name of a conquered people or city and topped by the image of a bound prisoner.

Such scenes were conventional in nature and often occur on temple pylons, because the pharaoh's earthly victories mirrored the triumph of the gods over universal chaos and depictions of them provided a powerful protection for the temple and its contents. However, Ramesses III was indeed a great war leader, who repulsed serious attacks on Egypt by "Sea Peoples" from the eastern Mediterranean and by Libyans from the west. After his reign the power of Egypt declined and her control over foreign regions contracted.

(Courtesy of J. Ruffle, University of Durham)

48
X-RAY OF THE SKULL OF RAMESSES VI

Ramesses VI died in 1134 B.C. amid a growing mood of civil strife at the end of the Twentieth Dynasty. References to this strife have been preserved in Papyrus Turin (2044), recording the burning of the people of the town Pet-nebyt; also an order to place guards at the pharaoh's tomb in case the trouble came closer to Thebes. Subsequently, the head of the *medjay* (the force policing western Thebes) told the foreman of the workmen building the tomb, "Do not go up (to the Valley of Kings) until you see what has happened."

A further indication of continuing trouble at Thebes was the fate of the mummy of Ramesses VI, which was literally hacked to pieces by tomb robbers shortly after its burial. When the priests of the subsequent Twenty-first Dynasty began their restoration work, they were forced in this instance to tie the dismembered parts to a rough piece of coffin board, and re-wrap everything most skilfully to create a semblance of the mummy form. A severed arm was re-wrapped on the thigh, and one hip bone was placed at the neck. The elbow had been cut with an axe, the neck severed from the body, and the face slashed repeatedly with a knife.

(Courtesy of James E. Harris, University of Michigan, Ann Arbor)

49
"DEMONS OF THE UNDERWORLD"
Valley of the Kings; from the tomb of Ramesses VI
20th Dynasty, *circa* 1135 B.C.

The texts and illustrations throughout this section
of the tomb are derived from various mythological
sources, including the "Book of Aker" (a composi-
tion dedicated to the two-headed earth-god of that
name) and perhaps also the "Book of Caverns,"
which was one of four descriptions of the geography of the underworld. Much of the work, however,
seems to have no previous parallel nor stimulus.

The theme of the painting is the "formation of a
new sun disc," and repeatedly we find various
enemies of the disc (which is identified with the
dead pharaoh) being destroyed by burning or decapitation. Their bodies are sometimes boiled in
cauldrons or devoured by demonic guardians of the
pharaoh; in adjacent scenes to that illustrated here,
their heads and their hearts have been placed in
fire-pits. In associated scenes, even the blood, the
internal shadow and the *ba* are cast upside down
into cauldrons to complete the destruction process.
Additionally, in the section of the painting below
the decapitation scene, there is a huge coffin containing a woman's body identified as "the corpse of
destruction." This scene is surrounded by other
gods and goddesses intent on destroying the pharaoh's enemies.

The content of this scene is typical of the much
increased emphasis placed upon the dangers of the

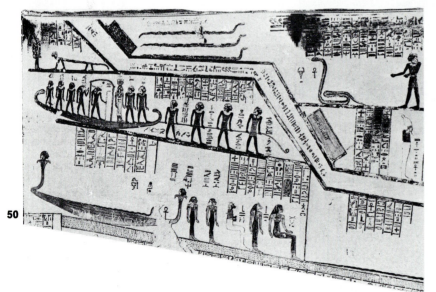

50

underworld in the funeral art of the late New Kingdom. It contrasts strongly with the confidence about the afterlife evident in the tomb decoration of the early New Kingdom and preceding periods.

(Courtesy of Bernard Fishman, Oriental Institute, Chicago)

50

"THE BOOK OF WHAT IS IN THE NETHERWORLD" (DETAIL)
Valley of the Kings; Tomb of Ramesses VI
20th Dynasty; 1134 B.C.

This "Book" described the passage of the sun-god in a barge along the river of the underworld. At first imagined as a dead ram-headed god, the sun-god undergoes mysterious experiences which result in his rebirth as a scarab beetle and ultimately as

the rising sun. Here his barge (central left) approaches the fourth region of the underworld, beyond which lies the tomb of Sokaris, where the sun-god's rebirth will begin. The serpents seen here are guardians of the sloping passage and its two open gates.

(*After* N. Rambova (edit.), 1954: *The Tomb of Ramesses VI,* plate 80. Pantheon Books, New York)

51

PAPYRUS WRITTEN IN HIERATIC
L., 0.61 m.
Thebes; this fragment is probably part of the British Museum papyrus 10383
20th Dynasty, *circa* 1100 B.C.

It is clear that the tombs of ancient Egypt were robbed persistently throughout antiquity. For example, Howard Carter recognized that ancient thieves made at least two attempts to loot the Eighteenth Dynasty tomb of Tutankhamun—first to remove the precious metal, second to gather the oils and ointments. Officials resealed the tomb and later rock and mud slides and rock chippings from work on a new royal tomb directly above were dumped on the tomb's entrance, preserving it hidden and undisturbed until its discovery in 1922. However, there is little written evidence about tomb desecration until late in the Ramesside period, when papyri describe how the robbers gained access to burial chambers, melted down the precious metals, and often burnt the bodies they had stripped.

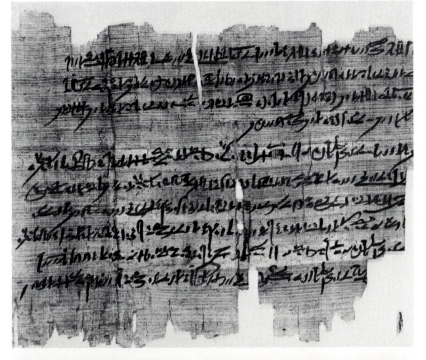

This particular papyrus reflects a closely related problem and contains part of a series of transcripts, reports and testimonies concerning objects stolen from a temple rather than a burial; reference is made to items in the Mortuary Temple of Ramesses II, the Ramesseum. Temple records were kept carefully throughout Egyptian history, and inventories of the ritual objects were made regularly. Damage and destruction, care and condition were observed and recorded, but it is not until the times of these papyri that we learn of the theft and successful recovery of these objects.

(University Museum: 49-11-1)

52

THE MUMMY OF AMUNHOTEP I (DETAIL)
Deir el-Bahri; the royal cache, found in 1881
18th Dynasty, 1524 B.C.

The son of Ahmose and Ahmose-Nefertiry, Amunhotep I became pharaoh in 1551 B.C. He married two of his sisters, Ahhotep II and Ahmose Meryet-Amun, and continued the stabilization of Egypt begun by his father after the expulsion of the Hyksos intruders (see **21**). Apparently in an attempt to protect himself after death, Amunhotep I atypically separated his mortuary temple from his tomb. The temple was erected at the edge of the cultivation at Thebes, was shared by his mother, and its location—unlike that of the tomb—is known. What is clear is that tomb robbers did find his burial and stripped it of all valuables. His badly battered mummy was one of the first to be restored by the Theban priests of the Twenty-second Dynasty, and placed into the secure Eighteenth Dynasty tomb of Queen Inhapi, in the cliffs of Deir el-Bahri.

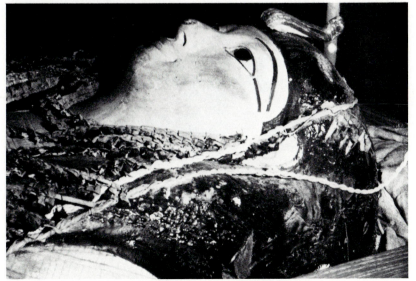

(Courtesy of James E. Harris, University of Michigan, Ann Arbor)

53
SHAWABTI FOR PHARAOH PSUSENNES I
Bronze
H., 0.083 m.
Provenance uncertain, probably Tanis
991 B.C., the time of the pharaoh's death

Next to that of Tutankhamun, the wealthiest royal burial to survive in Egypt was that of Psusennes I, the third pharaoh of the Twenty-first Dynasty. This burial was provided with more than 600 shawabtis, mainly in faience, but including at least a third in bronze. The choice of materials for these shawabtis, as well as for numerous other items in the burial (such as the coffin and the food vessels), suggests that a conscious effort was being made to avoid wood which would be perishable in the damp climate of the Nile Delta.

The rule of Psusennes I at Tanis gave him control of the trade between Egypt and the Mediterranean world, so his tomb furnishings in gold and silver reflect a quite substantial wealth. However, the division of political power in the Twenty-first Dynasty between Tanis and Thebes meant that no large-scale quarrying and building projects were feasible. Consequently, Psusennes' tomb was of modest dimensions, and made almost entirely out of stone plundered from the monuments of former pharaohs. The location of the tomb within the boundaries of the Tanite temple implies a greater concern for security, presumably in reaction to the damage done in the burials of the Valley of the Kings in the previous century.

(University Museum: 54-33-11)

54
SHAWABTI FOR THE ARMY COMMANDER AND HIGH PRIEST OF AMUN, PINUDJEM II OF THE 21ST DYNASTY
Blue faience
H., 0.18 m.
Thebes
969 B.C., the time of the priest's death

Pinudjem II was one of the last of the lineage descended from Herihor, who had established the effective independence of Thebes and Upper Egypt from royal control at the end of the Twentieth Dynasty.

When Pinudjem II died, his mummy was placed in the old tomb of Queen Inhapi, in the cliffs at Deir el-Bahri. Pharaoh Amunhotep I had already been moved to shelter in that tomb, and now the officials of the Theban cemetery became sufficiently confident about the tomb's security that they added the mummies of Seti I and Ramesses II. Within a few years, some forty other royal and priestly mummies were added to the cache.

(University Museum: E595)

55
WRITING BOARD OF NESKHONS
H., 0.29 m.
Deir el-Bahri, from the royal cache in the tomb of Queen Inhapi
Close to 974 B.C.

Neskhons was the wife of Pinudjem II (see **54**). This writing board, found among the burial equipment, is unique in that it contains a decree put in the mouth of Amun-Re' stating that the shawabtis of Neskhons would ". . . perform all the tasks for which shawabtis are made . . ." Additionally, they would, ". . . protect her every year, every month, every week, and every day . . ." The shawabtis were paid for with quantities of copper, cloth, bread, cakes and fish.

(Courtesy of the British Museum: 16672)

56
STATUETTE OF KAROMAMA
Bronze, inlaid with a feather design in gold, silver and electrum
H., 0.70 m.
Provenance uncertain, probably Tanis
22nd Dynasty, *circa* 835 B.C.

Karomama was queen to Takelot II of the Twenty-second Dynasty, centered at Tanis (945-715 B.C.). This dynasty opened with a revival of royal power, but subsequently was weakened by increasing problems. Its founder, Sheshonk I, was a leader of the descendants of Libyans who settled near Bubastis (in the Delta) after their defeat by Ramesses III several centuries earlier (see **47**). Sheshonk re-asserted royal power throughout Egypt by the installation of royal sons in key provincial posts, but this generated rival dynasties which competed with the sons of subsequent rulers for these positions. This led to open civil war in Karomama's times.

Sheshonk's aggressiveness against the Israelites in Palestine (see I, Kings 14, 25) faded as internal problems grew and as Assyria began to expand into the Levant. It was against this threat that Sheshonk's grandson Osorkon II eventually made an alliance with the Israelites.

(Courtesy of the Louvre Museum, Paris: AE020)

57
STELA FOR TA-SHERYT, CHANTRESS OF AMUN
Wood
H., 0.25 m.
Thebes; from excavations near the Ramesseum
22nd Dynasty, *circa* 900 B.C.

The chantress stands in adoration before Re' Horakhty, one of the forms of the sun-god, Re'. The god is seated before an offering table and holds a crook and a flail. The accompanying inscription includes a request for incense and linen for the deceased.

(University Museum: E2043)

58
CANOPIC JAR
Limestone
Height, 0.36 m.
Thebes; from the Ramesseum
22nd Dynasty, *circa* 900 B.C.

Canopic jars were originally fashioned to store the mummified remains of the internal organs of the deceased (see **33**). Here, the head of Imseti—the only one of the Four Sons of Horus to be in human form—is the top of the container. The inscription on the jar is dedicated to this god and mentions the deceased and his family. Through this inscription and the act of mummifying the organ (in this case, the liver), it and the mummy itself would survive into the afterlife.

By the Twenty-first Dynasty, since it had become the practice to return the mummified organs to the body cavity (see **66**), canopic jars were frequently dummies. However, such jars continued to be a common feature of the burial equipment and can be seen as symbolic gestures made by the deceased.

The inscription reads, "Osiris! Imsety! The House Mistress, the Noblewoman, the Musician of Amun-Re', in the Fourth Phyle, Nes-Netcheret justified, daughter of the prophet of Amun in Karnak, Har, and his mother, Ankhesenaset, justified."

(University Museum: E1869b/72a)

59
FIGURE OF PTAH-SOKAR-OSIRIS
Wood
H., 0.84 m.
Provenance uncertain, possibly Memphis
circa 850 B.C.

This figure was sculptured in the form of a mummy, and inscribed in hieroglyphs for the Osiris (i.e., the deceased) Syrt-Bast.

The custom of placing such figures as this one within the tomb began during the New Kingdom, though initially only the God Osiris was represented. They were often hollowed out to hold a rolled-up papyrus copy of the "Book of the Dead." However, after about 1000 B.C., the composite figure combining Ptah (the creator god of Memphis), Sokar (god of the Memphite necropolis) and Osiris, became popular, embodying the notions of creation, death and afterlife within a single deity.

The rectangular pedestals for these figures sometimes contain small pieces of the body itself (in addition to the papyrus), so that the base served as a symbolic coffin.

(University Museum: L-55-29)

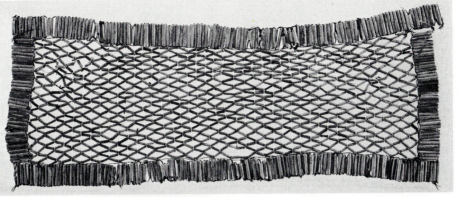

60

COLLAR THAT ONCE FORMED PART OF A BURIAL SHROUD
Pale blue faience beads
L., 0.36 m.
Thebes
circa 800 B.C.

The main apron of such a burial shroud was placed flat on top of the mummy, then curved about the body from head to toe. It was kept in position by cord ties. A bearded face similarly constructed of beads was placed over the face, and a collar like the one illustrated here was laid over the neck and shoulders. Several amulets were customarily associated with the use of this type of shroud: a winged scarab at the heart, figures of the winged goddess Nut, the jackal-headed Anubis, and the Four Sons of Horus, on the body below the collar.

(University Museum: L-55-90)

61

COFFIN OF HENETTAWY, A CHANTRESS OF AMUN
Wood
H., 2.03 m.
Deir el-Bahri, from the excavation of 1924 by H. E. Winlock, who was then director of the Egyptian Expedition of the Metropolitan Museum at Thebes
21st Dynasty, *circa* 1000 B.C.

This coffin was the larger of the two used for Henettawy's burial, one nested within the other. It is possibly one of the finest examples of Egyptian art of its period, though it interestingly has a number of details that are thought to have been copied from art styles of the New Kingdom, some three centuries earlier. In particular, the heavy earrings and massive wig (in life held on by application of beeswax and a series of head bands) were then the height of fashion among the ladies of the Theban court.

It was quite a common practice in the Third Intermediate Period to dispense with the effort of decorating the chambers of private tombs, and simply re-use older burial chambers. Henettawy's burial was no exception to this, her resting place being a plundered Eighteenth Dynasty tomb originally dedicated to a nobleman named Minmose.

This Henettawy, a girl of about 18 years when she died, should not be confused with the famous queen of the Twenty-first Dynasty of the same name (see **62**). Henettawy literally means "mistress of the two lands," and was one of the most popular names of her day. While her royal namesake was given an elaborate embalming treatment, this girl appears to have been simply bandaged and hastily buried very shortly after death.
(Courtesy of the Metropolitan Museum of Art, Museum Excavations, 1923-24; Rogers Fund, 1925: 25.3.182)

62

THE MUMMY OF HENETTAWY (DETAIL)
Deir el-Bahri: the royal cache, found in 1881
21st Dynasty, *circa* 1020 B.C.

Henettawy was a descendant of Herihor, who had founded a hereditary dynasty of Theban army commanders and High Priests of Amun which shared control of Egypt with the Tanite pharaohs of the Twenty-first Dynasty. Henettawy was the wife of Pinudjem I, one of the Theban dynasts; she herself held the impressive titles of ". . . Mother of the God's Wife of Amun, Mother of the God's Votaress of Amun, God's Mother of Khonsu the Child, the First Great Chief of the Concubines of Amun."

The techniques used in the mummification of Henettawy were almost exactly the same as those used for Nodjme (**66**), but the results were inferior. Her cheeks were so overpacked with a mixture of fat and soda that the face subsequently burst apart. Sawdust scented with aromatic oils was used to pack the abdomen. Fine linen was used in the wrapping, and her elaborate hairstyle was made of tightly twisted strands of black string.

(From G. Elliot Smith, 1912: *Catalogue Général des Antiquitiés Egyptiennes du Musée du Caire,* plate LXXV. [L'Institut Français, Cairo])

63

X-RAY OF MAKARE'
21st Dynasty, died *circa* 1000 B.C.

Makare', again a descendant of the Herihor lineage, apparently assumed an even more important role in the religious hierarchy at Thebes than earlier women in the dynasty. In a relief in the Khonsu temple, more elaborate than that of Henettawy, her headdress was titled, "God's Wife of Amun at Karnak," the highest status a woman could then achieve in the temple hierarchy.

Examination of the mummy of Makaré indicates she died at a relatively early age, and during childbirth, or shortly afterwards. The embalmers, using the subcutaneous packing method, appear to have attempted to emphasize that fact, by exaggerating the filling of the abdominal region.

(Courtesy of James E. Harris, University of Michigan, Ann Arbor)

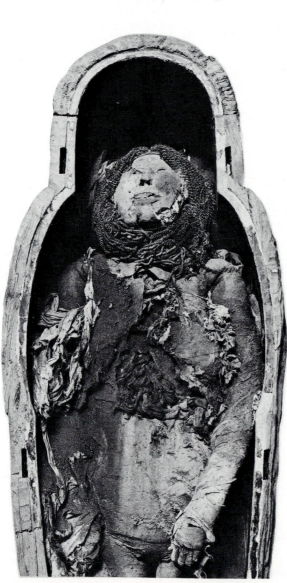

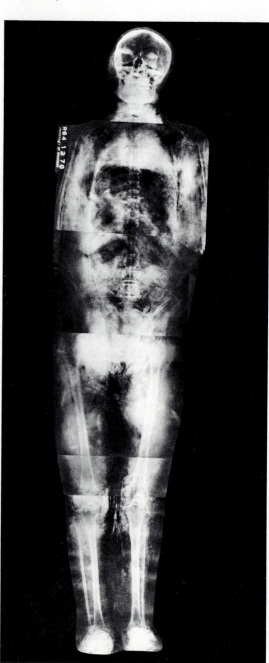

The reliefs from the chapel above the large tomb in which Satnubet lay, with other members of her family, show that they were wealthy; and Satnubet herself originally lay within three nested coffins, one of which had been elaborately decorated. (White ants had eaten away most of this woodwork, as well as the linen wrappings of her corpse.) As gifts, the burial had only four dummy canopic jars, two boxes of small mud shawabtis, a wooden figure of a funerary god, and a large pot. A winged scarab of flimsy plywood and a heart scarab of crudely prepared blue faience were placed on Satnubet's breast (**65**). A network of blue beads had originally covered the body, and a thin silver mouth-piece had been laid over the mouth; otherwise no jewelry (very common in New Kingdom and earlier burials) was found.

(Egyptian Section, University Museum)

64
BURIAL OF SATNUBET
L., 1.59 m.
Abydos, from a combined expedition of the University Museum (University of Pennsylvania) and Yale University
circa 700 B.C.

In the late New Kingdom and Third Intermediate Period important changes took place in the funerary practices of Egypt. Reflecting perhaps a different concept of the afterlife, objects of daily life were now rarely placed in the tomb and the funerary artifacts were often made of cheap materials, even those for wealthy burials.

65
BURIAL OF SATNUBET (DETAIL)
Abydos
circa 700 B.C.

Satnubet's two scarabs, as found *in situ,* on her breast.

(Egyptian Section, University Museum)

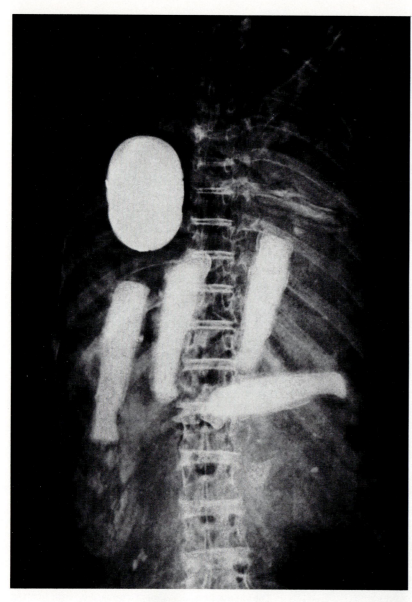

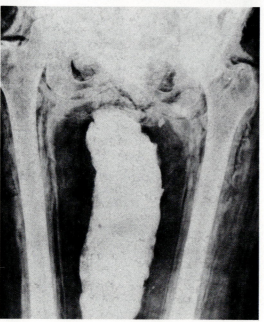

66
X-RAY OF QUEEN NODJME
21st Dynasty, died *circa* 1065 B.C.

At the end of the Twentieth Dynasty, *circa* 1080 B.C., as the Ramesside lineage was crumbling, a military commander, Herihor, took effective control of Thebes (and hence of Upper Egypt), and also became High Priest of Amun. Herihor was certain enough of his power to carve his name in a royal cartouche in temple reliefs and to precede it with titles formerly reserved for the pharaohs alone. But he did not depose Ramesses XI, then ruling at Tanis in the Delta; instead, he married his sister Nodjme. In so doing, he ensured that the position of High Priest would be filled by inheritance, not by royal appointment. One of the sons of this marriage, Smendes, was to become the first pharaoh of the Twenty-first Dynasty at Tanis in 1070 B.C.

Nodjme's mummy is the earliest known from this period of change, and it shows a number of major modifications in the embalmers' methods. There was a search for a portrait-like quality in the mummy, with packing filling out the face, artificial eyes inserted in the empty sockets, and red ocher applied to the skin to restore lifelike color. Since the time of Ramesses III (died 1151 B.C.) it had become the practice to return the viscera to the body cavity after it had been preserved, together with wax models of the four sons of Horus (see also **35**). These models, together with a large heart scarab amulet, stand out here in the x-ray of the thoracic cage.

This treatment just predates the introduction of the use of subcutaneous packing in mummification, as used for two of Nodjme's descendants, Henettawy and Makaré (see **62** and **63**, respectively).

(Courtesy of James E. Harris, University of Michigan, Ann Arbor)

67
X-RAY OF THE LEG REGION OF AN ELDERLY WOMAN NAMED BEKRENES
Sheikh Abdu'l Qurna
26th Dynasty, *circa* 7th century B.C.

Both the thorax and abdomen were tightly packed with bundles of linen and sand, in a way reminiscent of the embalmer's practices in the Twenty-first Dynasty some few hundred years earlier. However, the viscera were simply gathered up in two resin-soaked linen parcels which were placed between the thighs and the shins.

(Courtesy of the Trustees of the British Museum: 15654c)

68
GILDED COFFIN OF PADINEFERHOTEP
Wood
L., 1.75 m.
Hu (southern Egypt)
Ptolemaic Period, *circa* 3rd century B.C.

The box coffins of the Old and Middle Kingdoms were gradually replaced in the New Kingdom by anthropoid coffins imitating the form of the mummy itself. This lid of the cartonnage coffin of Padineferhotep is an example of the type. Such coffins often have richly colored scenes and decoration, but this one has been covered with a thin sheet of gold bearing incised designs; the gold is not only a sign of wealth but is also a reflection of the belief that, through ritual, the deceased was transformed into a being shining with light like the sun.

The scenes on the lid depict essential elements of

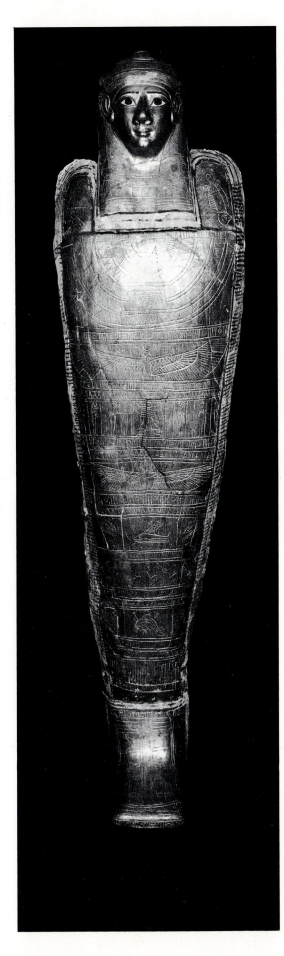

funerary belief. Isis and Nepthys appear on the wig lappets, reminding us that the deceased is literally to be identified with Osiris. A broad funerary necklace covers the breast, bearing a pectoral containing a heart, which in reality would have been inscribed with a spell preventing the heart from testifying to any sins at the judgment of the dead before Osiris. Below, Nut, the sky-goddess, receiver of the deceased's ascending spirit and symbol of the orderly universe, spreads her wings protectively across the mummy. Further down is a *djed*-pillar (see also **70**) flanked by funerary deities, and below this a winged scarab, representing the sun-god (with whom the deceased is identified) rising from the underworld. Underneath, we see the deceased as the mummy of Osiris being embalmed by Anubis while Isis and Nepthys watch. A register of funerary deities is followed by the *ba,* the form assumed by the deceased to move freely in and out of the tomb. The feet, like the face, are shown uncovered recalling that the "Opening of the Mouth" ceremony (see 44) has enabled the mummy to see, speak and move.

(University Museum: E4891)

69
X-RAY OF THE SKULL REGION OF A MAN, IDENTITY UNKNOWN
Provenance unknown
Style of preparation indicates a Ptolemaic date, *circa* 3rd century B.C.

Though the wrapping of the mummy itself was completed quite roughly, and finished with an over-liberal use of a black, pitch-like resinous material, the skeleton within is in good condition. However, the head was detached at the level of the sixth cervical vertebra, so that the brain could be removed at the *foramen magnum* rather than through the nasal cavities as was customary in earlier times.

(Courtesy of the British Museum: 29778)

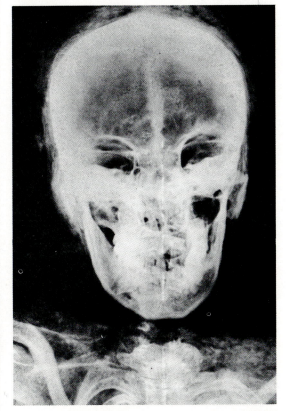

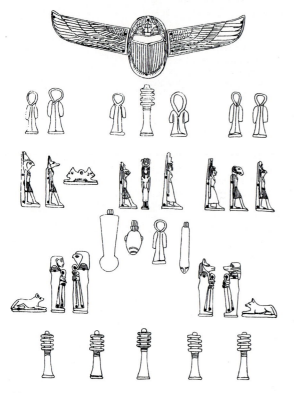

70

THE AMULETS OF DJEDHOR (SKETCH LAYOUT)
Faience (outer group) and various hard stones (inner group)
Abydos
Late Period, *circa* 380 B.C.

The mummy of Djedhor was found by Flinders Petrie during his 1902 field season at Abydos, in cemetery G which lies on the section of the desert running between the temple of Osiris and the great temples of the Nineteenth Dynasty, on the south side of the valley leading up to the royal tombs of the First and Second Dynasties. Djedhor's tomb, built *circa* 380 B.C., comprises two arch-topped rectangular chambers, the eastern one containing four sarcophagi (for Djedhor himself, his wife Nebtaihyt, and two people now unidentifiable); the west one, three sarcophagi for Djedhor's sons, Horwedjaef, Padieniset, and Padiusir.

Djedhor's mummy lay on a simple wooden tray, quite undisturbed, a group of green-glazed faience amulets set out on his breast, on top of the wrappings, almost as they were placed over two millennia ago. Subsequently, Petrie found a second group of amulets, sculpted in a variety of stones, and bound within the wrappings. Though a number of them were somewhat shifted from their original placement, he was able to suggest how they were probably distributed over the body. (There were also a number of ball beads lying among the amulets but their intended location could not be fixed.) Beneath Djedhor's head lay a bronze disc (a *hypocephalus*) covered with sketches of magical figures and numerous inscriptions, but without personal identification. However, an inscription on a smaller hypocephalus in the adjacent sarcophagus indicated that Djedhor, son of the lady Uza-au, was a priest of Osiris.

Each amulet had its specific purpose; many were protective—most obviously those of the gods; others were intended to aid in the deceased's revitalization in his afterlife, such as the *weres* amulet (in the form of a headrest) which would restore the head to life.

The symbolism and function of some of the more common amulets in the Djedhor group are listed below. Each amulet is a word in ancient Egyptian and carries its meaning for the deceased:

djed   In its early use in the Old Kingdom, this amulet probably represented the columns which supported the heavens, but in later interpretation it is equated to the vertebrae of Osiris. It means stability and endurance.

tyet   This amulet is the hieroglyphic word that means life or welfare. It is also the girdle of Isis and according to Chapter 156 of the "Book of the Dead," it is dipped in the juice of ankhamu (flowers), inlaid into sycamore wood, and put on the neck of the deceased.

ib   This amulet represents the heart with arteries as side projections. In one version of Chapter 29 of the "Book of the Dead," it is identified with the *ba* of Re' who leads the deceased to the afterworld. It was symbolic of the power of living and of human will-power.

wadjet   This amulet represents the Eye of Horus (see also 35), and when used in pairs, they were symbolic of the sun and the moon.

kheper   This amulet represents the scarab beetle sculpted in close detail. (See also 39 for a fuller discussion of this amulet's role in funeral ritual.)

(After Sir W. M. Flinders Petrie, 1902: *Abydos* I, plate LXXVIII. The Egyptian Exploration Fund)

71
WINGED SCARAB
Green glazed faience
L., 0.18 m.
Abydos; an amulet from the Djedhor group (**70**)
circa 380 B.C.

This amulet represents the sun-god Re', rising from the underworld.

(University Museum: E11384a-c)

72
THE DEITIES
H., approx. 0.045 m.
Abydos; amulets from the Djedhor group (70)
circa 380 B.C.

The deities represented are Khnum, Isis, Hathor, Horus and Anubis, respectively (left to right).

(University Museum: E11386 and E11388 to-91)

73
THREE AMULETS FROM THE DJEDHOR GROUP
Carnelian
H., 0.023 m. (*ib*), 0.021 m. (*kheper*), and 0.015 m. (*wadjet*)
Abydos; from the Djedhor group (70)
circa 380 B.C.

By 600 B.C., the functions of some important amulets vary somewhat, dependent upon the material used to make them as indicated in the different spells of the "Book of the Dead." Typically, the spell on the *ib* heart scarab, according to Chapter 26, was to be engraved on lapis lazuli, ". . . whereby the heart is given to a person in the underworld"; according to Chapter 27 the spell to be engraved on green feldspar was ". . . whereby the heart is not taken from him in the underworld . . ."; while Chapter 29 reads "Another chapter of the heart upon carnelian. I am the Heron, the soul of Re', who conducts the glorious ones to the Duat. It is granted to their *ba* to come forth upon the earth, to do whatsoever the *ka* wills . . ."

(University Museum: E11397, E11405 and E11416)

74
RELIEF OF CLEOPATRA AND CAESARION
WORSHIPPING THE GODS HATHOR,
HORUS SMATAWY, WENNEFER, HORUS OF
BEHDET, AND ISIS
Dendereh, from the rear wall of the temple of Hathor
circa 40 B.C.

The Ptolemaic dynasty continued the tradition of
foreign rule over Egypt established by the Persians;
after the death of Alexander the Great who had
conquered Egypt in 332 B.C., the country was taken
over by his general Ptolemy, whose descendants
ruled it until 30 B.C. The Ptolemies were Macedo-
nian in origin, spoke Greek as their native tongue
and made it a second official language. Greeks in
large numbers settled permanently in Egypt during
this time. However, traditional Egyptian culture remained strong, despite some obvious influences
from Greek art and ideas, and the Ptolemies maintained the age-old costumes and rituals of the
pharaohs. The Dendereh relief shows the famous
Cleopatra, the last adult member of the line, and
her son Caesarion, fathered by Julius Caesar. Wearing traditional royal costumes, they make offerings
to Hathor and other Egyptian deities. After Cleopatra's death Egypt was ruled directly by the Roman
emperors, but they too were depicted in Egypt as
traditional pharaohs and ancient Egyptian culture
persisted well into the Christian era.

(Courtesy of J. Ruffle, University of Durham)

75
BUST OF A MAN
Plaster
H., 0.66 m.
el Kharga
2nd century B.C.

During the Roman period of occupation of Egypt,
beginning *circa* 30 B.C., many immigrants were as-
similated into Egyptian culture, adopting Egyptian
religious beliefs and burial customs, including mummification. Consequently, this bust reflects the injection of several eastern Mediterranean influences
on an otherwise traditional Egyptian theme. In contrast with the impersonal cartonnage masks placed
on mummies from the Middle Kingdom onwards,
portraiture of the deceased was now realistic. The
general style is Hellenistic in nature, but the hairstyle and beard match the prevalent fashions of the
court in Rome.

The earlier types of this bust consisted of a hollow
headpiece which actually fitted over the skull. However, later examples, like the one illustrated here,
were raised at an angle to the body, to give the
impression that the head was resting on a pillow.

(University Museum: E886a,b)

76
PORTRAIT OF A YOUNG WOMAN
Wax colors on a wooden panel
H., 0.28 m.
er-Rubayat in the Fayum region
Late 2nd century A.D.

Panels of this kind represent the last stage in the development of the Egyptian ideal, to preserve the identity of the deceased in mummification. From early in the first century A.D., they were a popular substitute for the three-dimensional plaster masks of the Roman period.

In the portraits themselves, the dress is that worn everyday by the Roman elite. (The hairstyles and, to a lesser extent, the jewelry, help to establish their date.) The emphasis of the painting was always laid upon showing the deceased in youth or middle age, a characteristic echoing the idealization of representations in tomb paintings and sculpture during the early dynasties of ancient Egypt.

(University Museum: E16214)

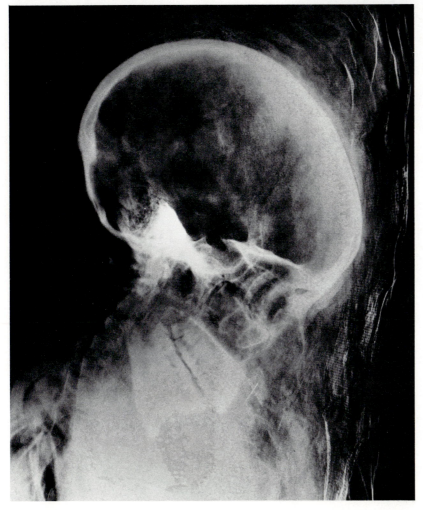

77
X-RAY OF THE MUMMY OF A YOUNG WOMAN
CALLED HERMIONE
Provenance uncertain, probably the Fayum region
2nd century A.D.

The head within the mummy wrappings is slumped forward, so that the front region of the skull serves as a back support for the portrait painted djrectly onto the outer linen's surface.

(Courtesy of Girton College, University of Cambridge. X-ray prepared by John Bashford, Department of Anatomy, University of Cambridge)

78

MUMMY OF AN ADOLESCENT BOY,
IDENTITY UNKNOWN
L., 1.32 m.
Hawara
1st century B.C.

Though the exterior bandaging is carefully exe-
cuted, x-radiography indicates that the body was
wrapped when it was already in an advanced stage
of decomposition. The ribs and spinal column are
in a state of utter confusion; the bones of the arms
were disarticulated and used as splints to
strengthen the regions around the thorax and pelvis; leg bones were laid outside the body to rein-
force this artificial structure.

(Courtesy of the Trustees of the British Museum:
13595)

79

MUMMY OF AN ADULT FEMALE
L., 1.66 m.
Fayum region
1st/2nd century A.D.

The body is enclosed in bandages coated with
resin. There is a painted and gilded cartonnage
cover, made up as several pieces for the head,
breast and feet. The breast cover was decorated
with imitations of serpent-bracelets, rings, neck-
laces inlaid with glass (to represent semi-precious
stones), and a bunch of flowers.

(Courtesy of Manchester Museum: 1766)

VII. HEALTH PATTERNS IN ANCIENT EGYPT

EGYPTIAN SOURCES

The ancient Egyptians were fond of their food and drink. This is clear in the scenes of banquet feasts in many tomb paintings, in the lists of offerings that accompanied the funeral ritual, and in the frequent representation of copious amounts of food heaped upon the table of offerings which was a focal point of tomb decoration from early pharaonic times. These sources, together with the numerous scenes of estate life in action, some models of rural activities (such as the making of dough, the slaughter of oxen, and the brewing of beer) and even remains of foodstuffs, allow us to begin reconstruction of the likely health patterns of the various levels of society in ancient Egypt.

For example, it is now established that barley was the principal harvest crop throughout the Old and Middle Kingdoms, after which time emmer wheat increased in importance, to become Egypt's main export in the Hellenistic period. Among the fruits, the fruit of the dom-palm, the date and the fig were most popular, and grapes for wine were grown in the Delta and close to oases. And, as a scene from the Nineteenth Dynasty Tomb of Ipy (at Thebes) amply illustrates, it was common practice to lay out a vegetable garden on the rich soil laid down by the Nile inundation and then raise a stream of water to it, using a bucket and counterpoise system called a shadūf. The herbs grown in these gardens supplied aromatic flavoring for wines and ingredients

Illustration 87

Text Figure 15
"PRODUCE OF THE WASTE LANDS"
Thebes; scene from the Tomb chapel of the vizier, Rekhmire'
18th Dynasty, *circa* 1450 B.C.

Servants on the nobleman's estate are shown bringing home animals, such as gazelle and rabbits, hunted on the fringes of the desert; and picking bunches of grapes to make wine.

After N. de Garis Davies, 1943: *The Tomb of Rekhmire' at Thebes II,* pl. XLV (The Metropolitan Museum of Art, Egyptian Expedition, volume XI.)

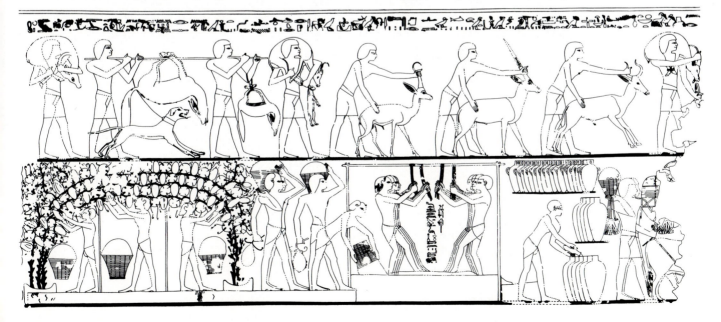

for various medicines.

Of a farmer's livestock, his cattle were the most valuable, serving as beasts of burden, as treaders of grain at harvest time, as a source of milk and, eventually, as meat (though this appeared only on the tables of the wealthy). In most of Upper Egypt grazing was poor and cattle had to be sent down to the richer pastures of the Delta for fattening, whereas sheep and goats could be maintained on the shrub at the desert's edge. Here too hunters could find oryx and gazelle.

Many estates maintained a stock of domestic fowl, such as geese, which were force-fed, but for everyone there was plenty of wild fowl to be trapped in the marshy fringes of the Nile's course, not to mention fish from the river itself. In all, we imagine the diet of the ancient Egyptians, with the exception of the very poor, was probably adequately balanced. Normality in infant tooth growth, and evidence of fatty deposits in arteries preserved in mummified tissue, generally support this claim.

In contrast, however, we have far fewer indications of how the ancient Egyptians judged their standards of health, or how they coped with sickness. Medical texts are few and generally fragmentary, among the most comprehensive being the *Edwin Smith Papyrus* which discussed the problems of cranial and chest injury at various levels of severity, and the broader *Ebers*

FARMING TERRACES ON THE WEST BANK OF THE NILE
Luxor

The Nile's waters were the mainstay of the economy of ancient Egypt (as they are of modern Egypt), since each autumn their flooding spreads fertile silt over the agricultural land of the valley floor. Crops of grain, fresh vegetables and fruits, together with a ready supply of fish in the Nile itself, assured all but the very poorest of the ancient Egyptians a reasonably healthy diet.

(Courtesy of J. Ruffle, University of Durham)

CALCIFIED EGG OF *SCHISTOSOMIASIS HAEMATOBIUM* IN LIVER TISSUE
(Magnification, approximately 150X.)
(Modern specimen taken in autopsy)

Parasitic infestation with *S. haematobium* was one of the serious health hazards for the Nile dwellers of ancient Egypt. In response to a chronic condition of *Schistosomiasis*, the body lays down calcium about the parasite's egg to seal it in. The calcified egg is extremely resistant to degradation (indeed far more so than the liver tissue itself) so specimens of it have been found in a well preserved state, during a number of recent histological examinations of mummified liver tissue. (See also **114**.)

(Courtesy of F. von Lichtenberg, Peter Bent Brigham Hospital, Boston, Mass.)

Papyrus which described concoctions to treat both external and internal diseases. Many things that could be attributed to obvious causes, such as malnutrition, were treated routinely enough, but often we can detect that illnesses were also regarded as a sign of a god offended, so that amulets and ritual spells formed part of the treatment. In the *Ebers Papyrus*, in particular, there is a very obvious dependence upon folk medicine (e.g., a mixture of sweet beer, goose grease, sycamore fruit and a variety of other ingredients, to overcome asthma), much of which is difficult to translate and difficult to interpret medically in terms of possible efficacy.

Additionally, tomb paintings and sculptures, since they usually portrayed the tomb's incumbent as he or she was in the prime of life (or sometimes in a generalized state of old age), rarely record physical shortcomings. The crippling effects of infantile paralysis are shown in the Stela of Roma; obesity and excess of fattening of the buttocks is uniquely recorded in a bas-relief of the Queen of Punt at Deir el-Bahri; dwarfdom is illustrated in both two and three dimensions, most notably in the Fifth Dynasty sculpture of the priest Seneb and his family in his tomb at Giza. But these examples stand out more by virtue of their abnormality than as any realistic expression of health patterns in ancient Egypt. It is at this point we must turn to data gleaned from the modern technical analysis of mummified remains, using x-radiography and autopsy.

Illustration 95

Illustration 94

Illustration 96

Illustration 106

THE HAZARDS OF NILE DWELLING

Whatever the source of the medical data, either bone or tissue, even a relatively superficial interpretation provides a constant reminder of the interplay between the ancient Egyptian and his environment. And here there is an irony, for just as the Nile was the bearer of fertility for the land which flanked it (and the backbone of Egyptian economy), so too it was the principal source of health hazards. The saturated soil harbored all manner of parasitic worms; the desert, which constantly tried to reassert itself during the dry season by encroachment on the cultivated areas, threatened men with disease due to the inhalation of fine sand particles during sandstorms.

The problem of parasitic infestation is readily illustrated by the common observation in mummies of schistosomiasis, the disease caused by the bilharzia fluke. Its calcified eggs have been detected in resin-preserved kidney tissue, and the irritation

Illustration 113

caused by its spiky ova has been detected by x-radiography as a calcification of the bladder region. Additionally over two columns of the *Ebers Papyrus* record diverse ideas on how to cure one of the standard symptoms of schistosomiasis, the presence of blood in the urine.

The worms that cause the disease (which is still widespread in Africa, India and the Far East) begin life in human blood vessels when pairs of flukes clinging to the vessel walls discharge eggs into the bloodstream. These eggs actually produce a chemical which can destroy small areas of the blood vessel's surface, and so they are soon able to gain access to the bladder or intestine, and so move on to the outside world. The survival of these eggs and their eventual development depend upon the fulfilment of a series of coincidences. They must land in fresh water if they are to hatch into larvae which, as they swim, must find one of a limited number of species of suitable snails upon which to lodge as they grow. These snails thrive in the still, sometimes stagnant canals which today, as in antiquity, took the Nile water away from the main stream to feed the fields used for crops and grazing.

Eventually the larvae, now matured into a fork-tailed form, leave the snail and swim on in search of a human host. Having penetrated the skin to enter the blood vessels, the parasites' growth is completed when they become flat bilharzia worms about a quarter of an inch long, firmly attached to their host's blood vessels once more. The delicate female is held protectively by the male until egg-laying begins the parasite's life cycle afresh.

Today modern medicine, both by direct attack on the bilharzia worms themselves (using a variety of drugs that can paralyze them and cause them to lose their grip on the vessel wall) and by disruption of the life cycle at the snail-hosting stage, is beginning to combat the disease. But in ancient Egypt there were no such remedies. Herdsmen wading across the canals to take their livestock to fresh pasture; the peasants working in the fields; paddling children, and even perhaps the nobles who hunted wildfowl in the marshes; all had to come into contact with the breeding grounds of this grim disease. The sufferer did not usually die swiftly, in part because human blood contains a small amount of a special white blood cell which actually attacks the worm. Instead he was destined for a life of increasing misery, perhaps some twenty years during which a general weakening of the constitution would have been linked to a growing mental inertia and physical lassitude. We can be sure schistosomiasis was a major killer in ancient times.

Of related diseases it suffices to note the similarity of the life cycles of their parasitic sources to that of the bilharzia worm, to appreciate that they too owed their im-

Text Figure 16
"HERDSMEN WADING"
Saqqara: scene from the Tomb chapel of Ti, a court official to pharaoh Neferirkare
5th Dynasty, *circa* 2510 B.C.

Herdsmen urge cattle across a canal or subsidiary river channel: the calf is carried to prevent it drowning. Such crossings were dangerous not only because of the dangers of infestation by parasites but also because crocodiles, now extinct in Egypt, were prevalent in ancient times.

After G. Steindorff, 1913: *Das Grab des Ti*, pl. 112. (Veröffentlichungen der Ernst von Sieglin Expedition: J. C. Hinrichs, Leipzig.)

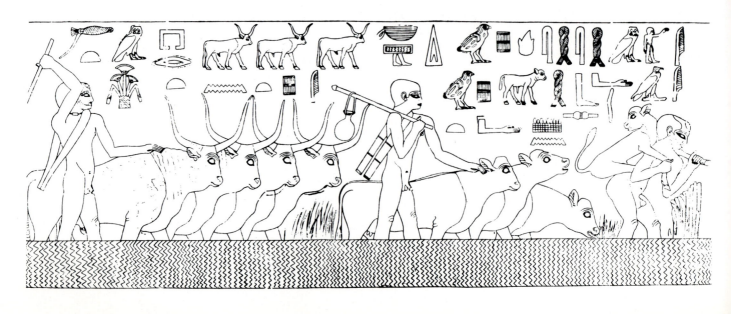

pact to the Nile's environment. *Strongyloides* contaminates wet soil and infests the intestines; *liver fluke* is hosted by a gastropod snail in its larval stages; *guinea worm,* once taken in as a contaminant of drinking water, attacks the abdominal wall and causes vicious ulceration of the legs. The impact and presence of all these parasites have been detected in mummified remains.

The hazard of the dry season was sand pneumoconiosis, a scarring of lung tissue very similar to that caused by coal dust inhaled during modern mining operations. Histological observation of this disease, using electron microscopy at magnifications of around 12,000x, is one of the most dramatic to come out of mummy autopsy. Because the mummification process was largely reserved for the wealthier sectors of society until very late in ancient Egyptian history, we lack many examples of pneumoconiosis, but it is not hard to imagine how serious a problem it would have been to the peasant farmers, often forced to weather a desert storm protectively close to their animals.

Similarly we find instances of *anthrocosis*—a buildup of carbon deposits in the lung tissue—among mummified remains, presumably because peasants and pharaohs alike kept warm close to wood fires. Again we can only surmise on how prevalent that disease was in some occupations of the poorer folk, such as closed-face quarrying or mining, lit only by fume-laden torches.

Illustration 115

GROWING OLD IN ANCIENT EGYPT

Many of the other health problems afflicting the ancient Egyptians have a familiar, modern ring to them: tuberculosis, inferred from the spine curvature it causes; arterial hardening, associated with advanced age; poliomyelitis, causing foot deformation; and degenerative arthritis, again often associated with older individuals, but sufficiently prevalent amongst younger people in their mid-twenties to suggest that it might have been caused by primary infections such as typhoid. Inevitably, there were skull fractures and broken limbs, some associated with war, some with occupational accidents, and some no doubt simply caused by domestic carelessness. There is also evidence of the arterial diseases which today are thought to be associated with psychological stress.

Where a sharp contrast can be made between the health of the ancient Egyptians and their modern counterparts is in their dentition. Today the sugar richness of

Illustration 100

Illustration 112

Text Figure 17
TOOTH ATTRITION
a, healthy tooth (in section); b, tooth damaged by the constant abrasion of sand particles caught up in bread and other foodstuffs.

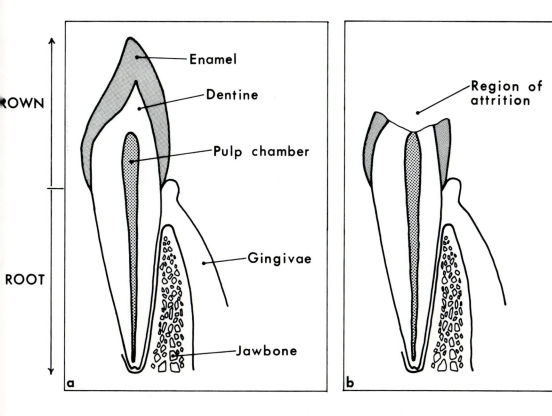

CROWN

ROOT

Enamel
Dentine
Pulp chamber
Gingivae
Jawbone

Region of attrition

a

b

diet—in Egypt itself somewhat heightened by the children's love of sucking sugar cane—has meant that *caries* (the development of cavities) is of major dental concern. But in ancient Egypt the diet was relatively sugar-free—although honey was used as a sweetener—so that caries had a relatively low incidence.

Illustration 91

The most striking feature of ancient Egyptian dentition is the extreme levels of tooth attrition. This is obvious from study of normal skeletal burials and from the various recent autopsies of mummies, but it can also be identified by a subtle adaptation of x-radiography, where a panoromic picture of the teeth and their supporting structures is laid out as an *orthopantomogram*. It appears that, so swiftly did tooth wear develop in most individuals that the normal protective mechanism, by which a secondary deposition of dentine replaces lost tooth fabric, was outpaced. As a result the pulp chamber (which houses the blood supply to the tooth) was partially exposed and bacteria could invade the root canal. If, subsequently, an abscess formed it could become the focus of infection that, at the very least, would have lowered the person's resistance to disease. In more severe cases, abscess invasion of the neck would have caused a singularly painful death.

Here again we are recording an interplay between the ancient Egyptian and his environment. Just as the fine particles of desert sand could be identified as the source of pneumoconiosis, so too those particles can be marked as the cause of tooth wear, being picked up as a contaminant by bread wheat as it was being harvested and winnowed. Add to that some grit from the grinding stones used in preparing the flour and even some sand which may have been deliberately mixed with the grain to speed up the grinding process, and the daily bread at once became a source of severe dental problems for all levels of Egyptian society, peasant and pharaoh alike.

The usual life span of an ancient Egyptian was about thirty-five to forty years, and we can now see that the last few years of that life were probably quite miserable, in health terms. We can speculate that he was at least spared the forms of cancer becoming increasingly prevalent in modern societies, and caused by chemical pollution of the air and water supplies. But in numerous ways he would succumb to disabling diseases closely related to his environment. He could not seek much relief from the medical world—the only known pain-relieving drug available was opium, but this could be afforded only by the wealthy—though some empirical treatments may have suppressed the worst of the pain; each disease, as it ran its course, had to be borne stoically until death.

80
CAT MUMMY
L., 0.46 m.
Provenance unknown, probably Bubastis
circa 2nd century B.C.

The cat-goddess Bastet, with her cult centered at Bubastis in the Delta, is recorded as an Egyptian deity as early as the Second Dynasty. But she achieved national prominence only when a Bubastite noble, Sheshonk I, became the first pharaoh of the Twenty-second Dynasty. By Classical times, the worship of Bastet attracted such fanatical devotion that living cats were treated with extraordinary reverence. For example, the Greek scholar Herodotus, writing in the fifth century B.C., observed that the owners of a cat would shave their eyebrows in mourning when the creature died. Additionally, Diodorus Siculus, when he visited Egypt in the first century B.C., witnessed the lynching of a Roman who had accidentally killed a cat.

A major feature of this worship of Bastet was the preparation of innumerable mummies of cats, to be dedicated to the goddess at her various shrines.

With this end in mind, cats were raised commercially and routinely killed (by breaking their necks) at the onset of maturity.

The cat mummy illustrated here, however, is very unusual, in that, despite the attention paid to the outward appearance of its wrappings there are no remains inside. Perhaps it served as an inexpensive substitute which was acceptable at the Bastet shrine as a real cat mummy.

(University Museum: 50-17-1)

81
X-RAY OF A CAT COFFIN
Wood
H., 0.46 m.
Provenance unknown
Late Period, *circa* 400 B.C.

As with coffins of humans, those of animals mirror the shape of the mummified creature within. The animal itself is actually only a kitten of the family *Felis silvestris libyca*.

(Courtesy of Manchester Museum: 9303)

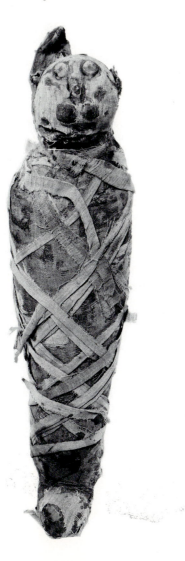

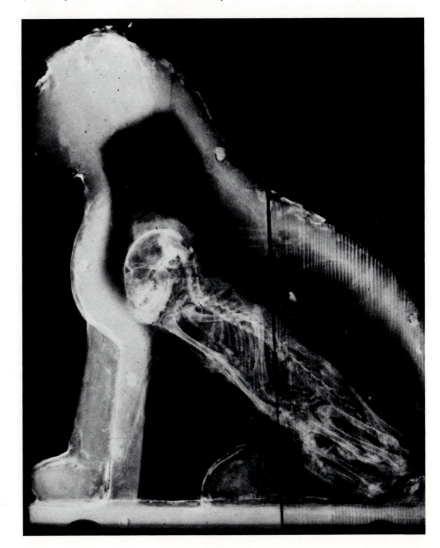

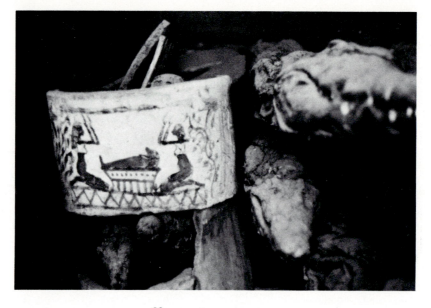

82

CROCODILE MUMMIES AND THEIR COFFINS
Temple of Kom Ombo
2nd century B.C.

The crocodile was the most feared animal on the Nile and understandably bore the title, "Lord of fear in the water." The menace of the crocodile was embodied in the crocodile-headed god Sobek, who was particularly revered in the Fayum region of Lower Egypt, and at Kom Ombo in Upper Egypt. The temple at Kom Ombo became a unique dual sanctuary where Sobek was worshipped alongside a form of the god Horus called "Horus the Elder," and where a pool of sacred crocodiles was an attraction of the site.

The more elaborate mummies of these crocodiles were given coffins of stone or clay. Here the figures of Isis and Nephtys are shown mourning, not Osiris, but an embalmed crocodile.

(Courtesy of B. Crowell, University Museum, University of Pennsylvania)

83

CROCODILE MUMMY
L., 0.69 m.
Fayum region
2nd century B.C.

84

X-RAY OF CROCODILE MUMMY

Crocodile cults were widespread throughout Egypt in the Graeco-Roman period, and the cult centers in the Fayum were particularly famous. Indeed, a papyrus letter has survived that requests the preparation of special cakes for a Roman dignitary who wished to feed the sacred crocodiles while visiting one of these centers.

The crocodile mummy illustrated here is of high quality in terms of wrapping, and is particularly interesting in that it was prepared over a bundle of three smaller crocodiles, none of which is the underlying structure for the carefully shaped muzzle region visible externally.

(University Museum: E12438. X-ray courtesy of the Xerography Unit, Hospital of the University of Pennsylvania.)

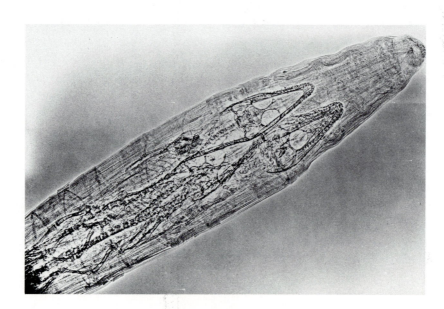

85

MUMMY OF AN APIS BULL
Provenance unknown, probably Saqqara
Ptolemaic, *circa* 2nd century B.C.

The Apis bull was the focus of attention of a cult at Memphis, from about the Fourth Dynasty onwards, at which time the creature was regarded as an incarnation of the supreme primordial deity, Ptah, who had created all other gods, including Re', by his own word. (Similar cults revering the Buchis and Mnevis bulls developed at Armant and Heliopolis, respectively, in honor of the war-god Montu and the sun-god Re'.) The bull, symbolic of strength and procreation, was luxuriously quartered in the temple of Ptah, to be led forth for public acclaim at certain festivals throughout the year, adorned with gold. Then, in death, the creature's body was embalmed in a conventional manner and given a funeral and rites of mourning which were almost as elaborate as those bestowed on the pharaoh himself.

From at least the Eighteenth Dynasty onwards, the dead Apis was buried just north of the Step Pyramid enclosure at Saqqara. The first archaeologically documented burials occur during the reign of Ramesses II. A great subterranean complex was developed and continued in use until Ptolemaic times. After *circa* 650 B.C. each bull was given a huge granite sarcophagus. Then, in the Ptolemaic period, when the Apis was regarded as the incarnation of Osiris also and was called "Serapis," i.e. Osiris-Apis and a truly national deity, pharaoh Nectanebos built the mortuary temple, called the *Serapeum,* close to Saqqara's Old Kingdom mastabas. In other galleries nearby, recent excavation has revealed the burial of Isis cows—the mothers of the Apis—and a vast number of mummified ibises, hawks and baboons.

(Courtesy of the Museum of Natural History, Washington, D.C.: 413941)

86

STELA FROM THE SERAPEUM
Limestone
H., 0.59 m.
Saqqara
Year 30 of Ramesses II; 1250 B.C.

This stela shows priests of Memphis carrying out the burial rituals for a deceased Apis bull, here represented as a statue standing in a wooden shrine (upper left). Before the bull two men, behind an offering stand, recite the ritual of the 'Opening of the Mouth' while below other priests hold up the ritual implements used in the ceremony.

(*After* M. Malinine, G. Posener, and J. Vercoutler, 1968: *Catalogue de Stèles du Sérapeum de Memphis,* plate 2. Musee Nationaux, Paris)

87

AGRICULTURAL SCENE FROM THE TOMB OF NAKHT, SCRIBE AND ASTRONOMER OF AMUN
Sheikh Abdu'l Qurna
circa 1420 B.C.

The rural settlements and field patterns of ancient Egypt are buried deep in water-saturated alluvium, and yet the nature of its agricultural life· is well known. Because much of life after death was believed to be a replica of that of the living in the Nile Valley, agricultural scenes (as well as many other aspects of daily life) were frequently depicted on the walls of each tomb chapel, from the Old Kingdom onwards. In the lower register Nakht surveys workers in his fields. Spaced along winding country lanes, they are breaking up the soil with picks, wooden mallets and plows; then they sow seed. One worker also chops down a tree with a short axe. In the upper registers grain is being harvested with sickles, then winnowed by tossing it into the air with scoops, so that the chaff is blown away. In between, Nakht's men measure the grain by means of a graduated container. Men like Nakht not only fed their families and workers from their harvests, but often had a surplus which they traded off for other commodities.

(*After* N. deGaris Davies, 1917: *The Tomb of Nakht at Thebes,* Plate XXI. Metropolitan Museum of Art, New York)

88

MODEL PICK
Wood
L., 0.30 m.
Deir el-Bahri, from a foundation deposit from the mortuary temple of Queen Hatshepsut
1483 B.C.

Agricultural and other tools rarely survive, but models of them are not infrequent. This miniature pick (made of wood like real picks and hoes in ancient times), along with similar models of other implements, some magical emblems and some of the materials used in the construction of the temple itself, were deposited in pits on the site, as a kind of memorial to the royal builders.

(University Museum: E1037)

89
SPORTING IN THE MARSHES
Sheikh Abdu'l Qurna, from the Tomb of Nakht, Scribe and Astronomer of Amun
circa 1420 B.C.

Attended by his family, the nobleman hunts ducks with a throwing stick (see **90**), and spears fish—though the artist forgot to include the spear. (A goose once appeared on each papyrus skiff, and a cat in the bushes, but for some reason these have both been defaced.)

(Courtesy of the Metropolitan Museum of Art, New York: 15.5.19e)

90
THROW-STICK
Wood
L., 0.68 m.
Meydum
18th Dynasty

This is a rare example of the throw-sticks used by the Egyptians as seen in scenes such as that above; they are efficient and formidable weapons.

(University Museum: 31-27-226)

91
MODEL OF DOMESTIC ACTIVITIES IN EGYPTIAN
DAILY LIFE
Wood
L., 0.70 m.
Beni Hasan, from the Tomb of Khnum-Nakht
12th Dynasty, *circa* 1850 B.C.

The basic foodstuffs of ancient Egypt are shown
being prepared. On the left, two women grind grain
on stone slabs; later it will be used to make nu-
tritious—but debris-filled—bread. On the right, beer
—a staple drink—is being fermented. In the center
an ox is being slaughtered; for most Egyptians meat
was a luxury item that was only rarely consumed.

(Courtesy of Merseyside County Museum, Liverpool:
55.82.7)

92
MODEL GRANARY WITH FIGURES WORKING ON
STARCH WHEAT (*EMMER*) OR BARLEY
Wood
L., 0.37 m.
Sedment, from the Tomb of Khentkhety
circa 2100 B.C.

As the climate of Upper Egypt is virtually rain-free,
the walled granary is unroofed. Two figures stand
in the lower area, their ankles covered by loose
grain; one of them scoops up the grain in a measure (probably a *hekat* which is a little over a gallon
in capacity) to fill the sacks. The sacks themselves
are lifted upstairs, to be emptied into storage bins.
An overseer supervises the measurement of the
grain, and a scribe, with a writing board and ink
palette, records the process.

A near-contemporary papyrus documents that a
field-hand would receive five measures per month,
which is equivalent to a daily intake of 1500 calo-
ries. This was scarcely an adequate diet in itself,
but, as the same document tells us, these were
hard times in Egypt and these workers should be
grateful for their meager fare.

(University Museum: E14259)

93
SKULL OF A MAN
H., 0.21 m.
Tell el-Yudiyeh (eastern Delta)
20th Dynasty, *circa* 1150 B.C.

The linen bandages that once covered this mummified head have rotted away to fully expose the extremely worn teeth still remaining in the deceased's
mouth.

(University Museum: E3354)

94
STELA FOR ROMA, THE DOORKEEPER FOR THE LADY YAAMIA
Wood
H., 0.27 m.
Saqqara
Late 18th Dynasty, *circa* 1300 B.C.

The stela is exceptional in its depiction of a deformity in the deceased, in this instance the leg-withering associated with poliomyelitis. The principal inscription reads: "A boon which the pharaoh gives and which Astarte of Syria gives, the Lady of heaven, Lady of the two lands, mistress of gods, (consisting of) happiness and joy, and a beautiful burial in the western necropolis of Memphis for the *ka* of the doorkeeper Roma."

(Courtesy of Ny Carlsberg Glyptothek, Copenhagen: 134)

95
EBERS PAPYRUS (FIRST LEAF)
H., 0.30 m.
Provenance unknown
18th Dynasty, *circa* 1540 B.C.

In several places the papyrus describes itself as a "compilation," and there is much evidence to show that it is a copy of various ancient works. For example, reference is made to the blood vessels of the body in a book that mentions a king of the First Dynasty. However the compilation was carefully planned, care being taken to cover the most diverse diseases which a physician should treat. Little is said about surgical problems, such as wounds or fractures: instead, prescriptions are presented for cure of internal and external symptoms of ill health, such as vomiting, discharge of blood and severe diarrhea.

The entire text is distributed over 108 columns. The opening one illustrated here supplies a couple of recitals that had to be made before medical treatment could begin: one, ". . . for applying a remedy to any man . . .", the other, "for loosening any bandage . . ."

(*After* L. Stern, 1875: *Papyrus Ebers,* plate 2. Wilhelm Engelmann, Leipzig.)

96

THE MUMMY OF DJED-HAPI

L., 1.76 m.

Provenance unknown

Third Intermediate Period, *circa* 750 B.C.

From the inscription on the lid of the coffin of this mummy (see Frontispiece) we know that Djed-Hapi was the son of a man named Petosiris and a woman named Sermuthepet, but there is no indication of Djed-Hapi's status in Egyptian society. Pieces of cartonnage were placed on the mummy before it was deposited in the coffin. The piece at the breast shows, in its lower section, Isis and Nepthys mourning the mummy of Osiris (equated with the deceased), while the sky-goddess Nut spreads her wings protectively over the scene. In the upper section there is an elaborate funerary necklace topped by a human-headed vulture—an unusual representation of the deceased transformed into a *ba*. A lower piece of cartonnage bears similar scenes, while yet another covers and represents the feet of the deceased.

(University Museum: E3413)

97a

X-RAY OF DJED-HAPI'S HEAD

Frontal View

The head and cervical spine are severed completely at the C6-C7 level in the vertebral column. The teeth are in a poor state of repair and several of them appear to have been knocked out in the postmortem period and displaced to the upper part of the throat.

(Courtesy of the Radiology Department, Hospital of the University of Pennsylvania)

97b

X-RAY OF DJED-HAPI'S HIP REGION

Frontal View

(Courtesy of the Radiology Department, Hospital of the University of Pennsylvania)

98

X-RADIOGRAPHY OF DJED-HAPI

Hospital of the University of Pennsylvania; May 18, 1980

The structure of Djed-Hapi's mummy, underlying what appears to be some twenty layers of linen wrapping, was determined by a series of twenty-two x-radiographs covering the length of the body. From the minor degree of the lateral curvature of the spine (*scoliosis*), and from the degenerative changes in the vertebrae and both hip joints (**97b**), it would appear that Djed-Hapi died in his 50's, perhaps even a little later.

Very much in keeping with the simpler embalming practices of the latter part of the Third Intermediate Period, the body cavity contains no visceral packages (contrast the treatment of queen Nodjme some three centuries earlier: **66**), and there is no subcutaneous packing of the body's surface (contrast this to the treatment of Makare': **63**). The cranial vault is intact and there is no sign of any fracture of the bone at the rear of the nasal region (**97a**), as we would have expected if the brain had been extracted in that manner (see **32**). Indeed a dense patch in the x-ray of the rear of the vault may be the remains of the brain which dried out naturally during burial.

The most striking feature of this x-ray study is the state of the neck of the body. The head is separated

cleanly from the body without any fragmentation of the vertebrae (arrowed in **97b**). Presumably this separation was made deliberately after Djed-Hapi died—the offset construction of the covering headpiece indicates that the embalmers were aware of the head's displacement—but why it was done is uncertain. The mummy fits so snugly into its coffin, it is tempting to suggest that the embalmers realized, in advance, the body would have to be shortened. However it may be that the separation was simply the first step of a planned, but never completed, removal of the brain via the base of the skull, as became routine in Ptolemaic times (see **69**).

(Courtesy of Michael Wakely & Associates, Philadelphia)

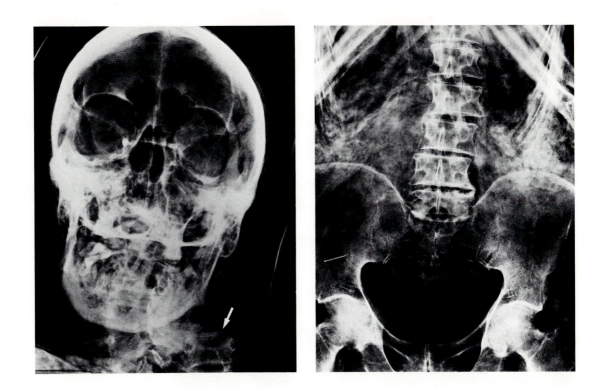

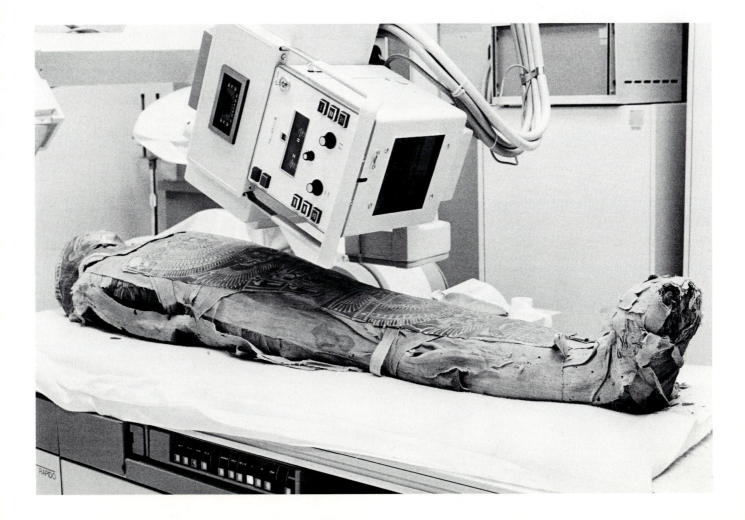

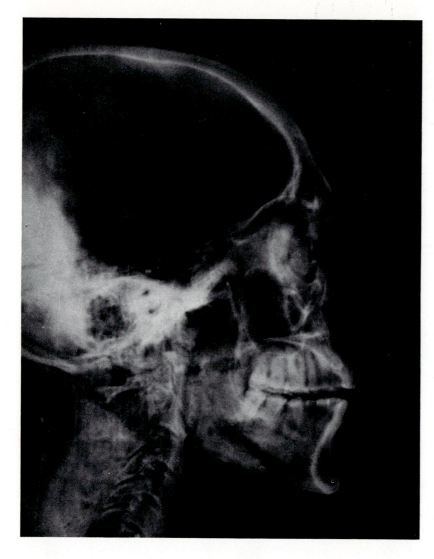

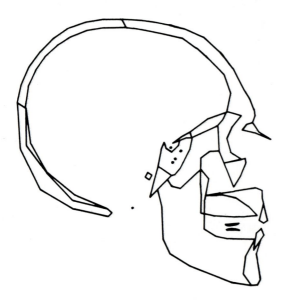

99

X-RAY OF THE SKULL OF SETI I AND CRANIAL RECONSTRUCTION
19th Dynasty, died 1279 B.C.

Perhaps the most impressive use of x-radiography for the analysis of mummies is that of Prof. James E. Harris and his staff while working on the royal mummies in the Cairo museum. Apart from indicating the diverse ways in which the pharaohs and their family members were embalmed (see Makaré and Nodjme, in **63** and **66**, respectively), and much about the abuse of the mummies by tomb robbers (see Ramesses VI, in **48**), this research has revealed, in remarkable detail, their state of health during life. For example, a deformity in one of pharaoh Siptah's feet indicates that he suffered from polio-myelitis (**94**). Additionally close analysis of various regions of the body of Ramesses II reveals such problems as arteriosclerosis, arterial hardening, and extreme tooth wear, all consistent with that pharaoh's advanced age of about ninety years at death (**101**).

Emphasis has been laid upon the lateral x-radiography of skulls, since this allows the principal features of the bone structure to be summarized by computer graphics. Intercomparison of the bone features indicates extreme diversity among the New Kingdom pharaohs and their queens. An interesting exception to this generality is the very close physical similarity of Amunhotep II (died 1419 B.C.) and his successor Tuthmoses IV.

This method of cranial reconstruction has also been used on a previously unidentified mummy found in the royal cache in the tomb of Amunhotep II at Deir el-Bahri' to suggest it is that of Queen Tiye. Her skull structure closely relates to those of her parents Yuya and Thuya (see **36**). Identification was completed by comparison of trace impurities in a strand of hair taken from the mummy with those in hair from a locket found in a small wooden coffin inscribed for Queen Tiye and placed in the tomb of Tutankhamun.

(Courtesy of James E. Harris, University of Michigan, Ann Arbor)

100
X-RAY OF THE FOOT OF SIPTAH
19th Dynasty, died 1187 B.C.

(Courtesy of James E. Harris, University of Michigan, Ann Arbor)

101
X-RAY OF RAMESSES II
19th Dynasty, died 1212 B.C.

(Courtesy of James E. Harris, University of Michigan, Ann Arbor)

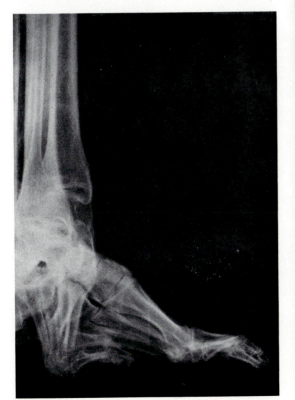

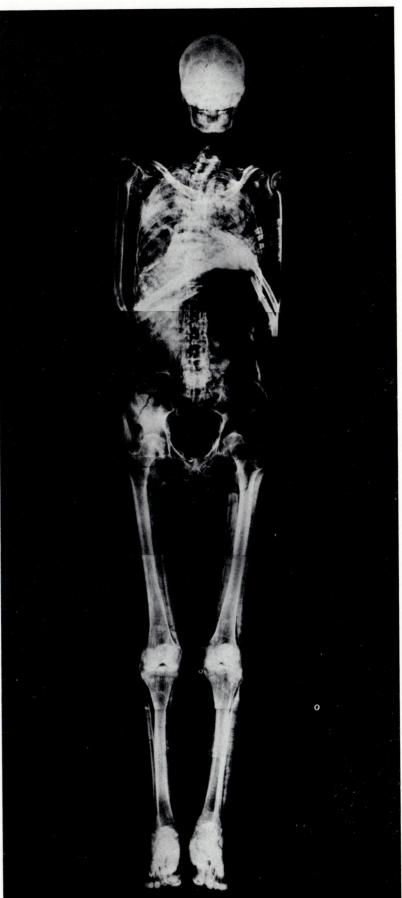

102

THE MUMMY HAPI-MEN AND THE REMAINS OF ITS
DAMAGED CARTONNAGE BREAST COVER
L., 0.62 m.
Abydos, Cemetery G
Ptolemaic, *circa* 3rd century B.C.

The tomb of Hapi-Men was excavated by Sir
Flinders Petrie in 1902, in cemetary G at Abydos.
He observed that it was quite different from any
other in the cemetery since the sarcophagus was
placed in the space between two other tomb chambers, and had a brick recess added either side of
it to take the tomb furniture. In one recess, there
was a box of thirty-three shawabtis, one inscribed
on the front, for Hapi-Men. On top of this box were
placed a pair of Osiris figures and a wooden hawk.
In the other recess there was a canopic chest
painted with great detail, and containing two long
packages of natron, together with a figure of
Nepthys, sister of Isis. Unfortunately, all of the
woodwork was almost completely ruined by the
attack of white ants.

Within the outer rectangular stone sarcophagus was
one of human form. Its face was rather poorly
painted (except about the eyes), and the front was
engraved and painted with a collar and an inscription which requests Osiris to grant the usual offerings to the *ka* of "... the third Priest of Mut, ...
the Priest of Horus, the Osiris Hapi-Men, true of
voice."

Both of the sarcophagi had been broken through at
the side and the mummy had been torn open over
the breast by ancient plunderers in search of amulets. A decorative cartonnage that would have
originally covered the length of the body was badly
damaged at that time, so that only the chest pectoral and the foot-casing remain.

An unusual feature of Hapi-Men's burial is that a
small mummified dog, carefully wrapped in linen,
was placed at the side of the man's feet.

(University Museum: E16220)

103

X-RADIOGRAPHY OF HAPI-MEN
Hospital of the University of Pennsylvania; May 18,
1980

The details of the internal structure of the mummy
of Hapi-Men were determined by a series of sixteen
x-rays covering the entire length of the body. On
the basis of the minor degree of degenerative
changes in the lower region of the spine it was
estimated that Hapi-Men was probably in his 40's

when he died.

The embalming treatment included a conventional removal of the brain through the nasal passage, with the cranial cavity being partially refilled with resin (**105**). There are no visceral packages in the body cavity, though on each side of the lower chest and upper abdomen there are near-cylindrical objects that may represent rolls of cloth. (An intriguing alternative possibility is that they are rolls of papyri.)

The x-ray of the chest (**104**) shows the care with which the looter, who broached Hapi-Men's coffins, treated the mummy itself, the penetration on the upper left side causing no damage to the deceased's rib-cage. There are several fingers missing on the right hand, but the body is otherwise in a good condition of preservation. (Contrast can be drawn with the way in which pharaoh Ramesses VI was treated by tomb robbers: see **48**.)

It is clear what the looters were seeking: amulets of precious metal. The confused condition of the amulets at Hapi-Men's throat, and the way that the wire on which they were threaded now lies twisted high on the body's right side, suggest that a thief reached under the wrappings and snatched a valuable item away from a necklace which was originally wrapped close to the front of the mummy.

(Courtesy of Michael Wakely & Associates, Philadelphia)

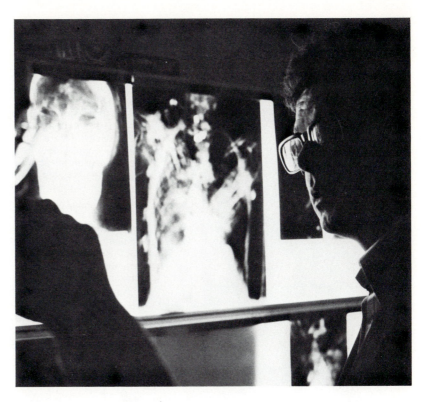

104
X-RAY OF HAPI-MEN'S BODY
Frontal view

Amulets which are identifiable in this view are: a, an *ib* (the heart); b, a *kheper* (scarab beetle); c, a pair of *wadjet* eyes; d, a group of *djed*-pillars; and e, a group of figurines, probably the four Sons of Horus. (For amulet descriptions see **70**.)

(Courtesy of the Radiology Department, Hospital of the University of Pennsylvania)

105
X-RAY OF HAPI-MEN'S SKULL
Lateral view

Note the amulet held in the linen wrappings at the forehead. An x-ray taken as a frontal view of the skull indicated it was a *wadjet* eye (see **35**).

(Courtesy of the Radiology Department, Hospital of the University of Pennsylvania)

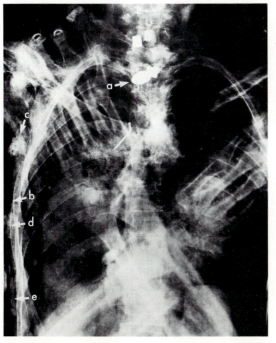

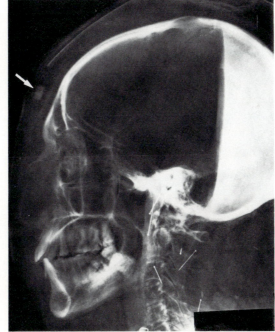

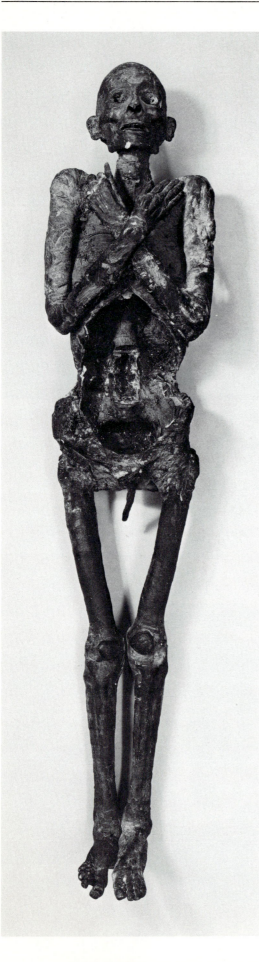

106a
THE BODY OF PUM II, AFTER AUTOPSY
L., 1.67 m.
Provenance unknown
Ptolemaic period, *circa* 170 B.C.

PUM II (Pennsylvania University Museum II), so named because he was otherwise anonymous and was the second mummy from the University Museum's collection to be autopsied, was judged to be Ptolemaic in date, both on the basis of the nature of his linen wrapping (see Front Cover of this volume) and on an age determination of 170 B.C. ± 70 years (P-1884), obtained by radiocarbon analysis of a portion of those wrappings.

Measurement of the mummy's length suggested that the coffin in which PUM II was found was the original one (cf. the situation for so many of the royal mummies in the Deir el-Bahri cache—see **48** and **52**). But the absence of any name for the deceased on the coffin lid would indicate that the coffin was taken "from stock," not custom-made.

When the body of PUM II was unwrapped for autopsy, its color was a light brown. However within a day of exposure to air it had darkened appreciably. Today the remains are almost black.

(University Museum L-55-15)

106b
THE BODY OF PUM II, AFTER AUTOPSY (DETAIL OF FEET)

(Courtesy of the Detroit Institute of Arts, Detroit)

107
AUTOPSY OF PUM II IN PROGRESS
Wayne State University School of Medicine, Detroit: February 1, 1973

The mummy was prepared with about twelve layers of linen wrapping of varying qualities of cloth. Hot liquid resin had been poured liberally over the body at many stages of the embalming process, so that access to the body itself involved a lengthy initial period of chiselling the mummy's surface. However the body within was in a fine state of preservation. On the basis of anatomical studies the age of the individual was estimated at between 35 and 40 years. Inside the abdominal and thoracic cavities were four packages, one containing spleen and some intestine, the other three containing portions of lung. Some of the aorta and a piece of heart tissue were preserved in the body cavity by a liberal coating of hot resin which had been poured over the packages and the floors of the thorax, abdomen and pelvis. Nothing remained of the kidneys or of the urinary bladder.

The outer surfaces of all the packages were found to be covered with pupae of insects which have specialized to breed in decaying flesh. They included the "cheese skipper" (*Piophila casei*) and the blow-fly (possibly *Chrysomya albiceps*) (see **108**). Additionally the remains of an adult beetle (genus *Dermestes*) were found in the vertebral column. All these insects must have attacked the body of PUM II while the embalmers were eviscerating the body cavity, and though some may have survived being covered with natron dessicant they were finally trapped and destroyed by the subsequent application of resin. A similar fate befell the larva of a beetle of the species *Staphylinidae* which had worked its way into the canal of the left eardrum.

Examination of the intestinal tissue revealed the presence of a partially digested fragment of meat fiber, and an egg of the parasite, roundworm (*Ascaris*). (See **109**, and compare the life-cycle of this parasite with that of *Strongyloides* discussed in **115**.)

The lung tissue contained patches of fiber damage, with inclusions of carbon and silica, that caused anthrocosis and pneumoconiosis respectively (see **111** and **112**). The aorta and other vessels from PUM II were in excellent condition, so that it was possible to detect the build up of fibrous material (*plaque*) on the wall of the aortic vessel and the fibrous thickening of the arteries, associated with the diseases, atheroma and arteriosclerosis, respectively.

PUM II was x-rayed prior to the autopsy and a number of bone abnormalities had been noted. The most interesting of these was the swelling of the right leg which, in autopsy, was identified as an inflammation of the connective tissue around the bone structure. The cause of this inflammation is unknown, but it could have been due to some chronic condition such as varicose veins. The displacement of the toes of the same leg (**106b**) was identified as an effect of the tightness of bandaging during mummification, not the result of any disease.

(Courtesy of the Detroit Institute of Arts, Detroit)

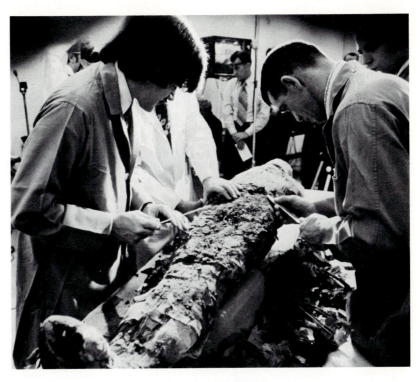

108
SCANNING ELECTRON MICROGRAPH OF A BLOW-FLY LARVA ►

Puparial stage of development (possibly of *Chrysomya albiceps*)

(Courtesy of P. K. Lewin, Hospital for Sick Children, Toronto)

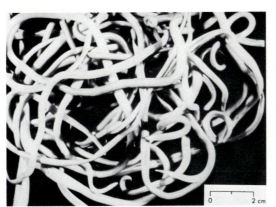

109
ADULT WORMS OF *ASCARIS LUMBRICOIDES*
Modern specimen

Ascariasis is a parasitic infection affecting the small intestine. It is a disease that thrives in overcrowded rural communities where sewerage is primitive or inadequate. Contamination of soil by human feces is a key factor in the spread of the infection. In ancient (as in modern) Egypt the infective eggs of the *Ascaris lumbricoides* mature readily in the warm, moist and shady soil of the cultivated terraces on the Nile bank.

(Courtesy of the Department of Parasitology, University of Pennsylvania)

110
SCANNING ELECTRON MICROGRAPH OF THE BEETLE LARVA *STAPHYLINIDAE*
L., approx. 1.5 mm.

(Courtesy of G. E. Lynn, Wayne State University School of Medicine, Detroit)

111
STONE-WORKER'S MALLET
Wood
L., 0.31 m.
Deir el-Bahri
18th Dynasty, *circa* 1400 B.C.

Perhaps the most unhealthy occupation in ancient
Egypt was working in the quarries which supplied
the stone for the monumental architecture such as
the pyramids at Giza and the temples at Luxor.
Whether it was in the limestone quarries of Tura in
the north, or the sandstone quarries of Gebel
Silsileh in the south, the working conditions must
have been most unpleasant, with dust constantly
swirling in the air. That dust, unlike the age-worn
sand of the desert, was angular and abrasive, and
caused chronic conditions of scarring in lung tissue
(*silicosis*). Artisans too, such as those who carved
out the cliff temple of Ramesses II at Abu Simbel,
were exposed to this progressively disabling disease.

The mallet illustrated here is the most familiar of
the artisan's tools, with the region of the head used
to strike a bronze chisel being heavily scarred and
worn away, by hard use day after day.

(University Museum: E2434)

 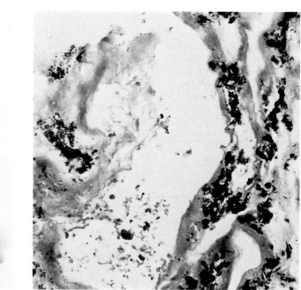

112

ANTHROCOSIS IN LUNG TISSUE
Magnification, approx. 200X

Besides the damage done to the lungs either by the
fine sand swirled up in a desert storm or by the
stone grit produced during quarrying (**111**), there
was also the risk of *anthrocosis,* i.e. the impregna-
tion of lung tissue by fine carbon particles. This is
a disease familiar today among coal-mining communities in the industrialized western world, but in
the case of the Egyptians the cause must have
been the fumes of the oil lamps used to light their
homes, and of the fires used for cooking.

(Courtesy of P. J. Turner, Department of Pathology, East Birmingham Hospital)

113

PAPYRUS PLUCKING
Saqqara: The Tomb of Nefer
circa 2420 B.C.

Modern medical research suggests that *schistosomiasis* can be combatted using a variety of chemo-
therapy techniques. For example, the injection of
special white cells (called *eosinophil*) into the blood
stream results in direct damage to the *schistosome's*
skin and eventually causes the parasite's death.
However, no such treatments were available in ancient Egypt, so the disease was readily maintained
by the Nile dwellers who had to wade in the river
itself or in the irrigaton canals running off it.

(Courtesy of D. Silverman, University Museum, University of Pennsylvania)

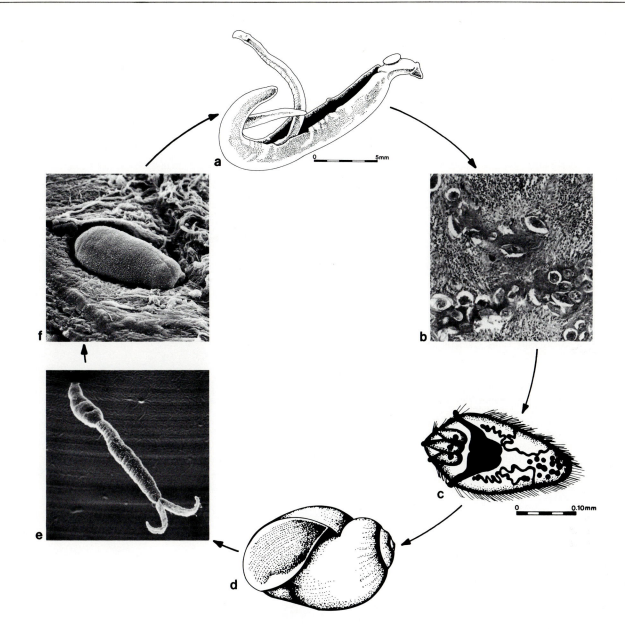

114

THE LIFE CYCLE OF *SCHISTOSOMIASIS HAEMATOBIUM*

Schistosomiasis haematobium is a human parasite which must have been a major source of poor health in ancient Egypt:

a. Pairs of *schistosomes* cling together in the veins of the bladder, the female worm cradled in a groove running the length of the male's body.

b. The female worm, once fertilized, deposits eggs in the wall of the bladder, so that they are subsequently discharged with the host's urine. (A small number of eggs are carried by the blood stream, back past the worm-pair, to become trapped in the liver—see Color Plate page 70.)

c. The first larval stage (*miracidium*), as they swim, have only a few hours to find and penetrate a suitable water snail, to continue the life cycle.

d. In the Nile Valley the principal carrier of *S. haematobium* is the snail *Bulinus truncatus.* The *miracidium* penetrate the exposed soft tissue of the snail, convert to a new form called a *spora-*

cyst, which moves onwards to the snail's liver. Within two weeks the liver tissue is almost entirely destroyed, but hosts huge numbers of the next larval stage, the *cercariae.*

e. Soon the fork-tailed *cercariae* escape from the snail in swarms, and swim on in search of a human host. They have a life-span of some two days.

f. As the *cercariae* penetrates human skin it sheds its tail, to become a *schistosomule. The schistoso mule* continues to burrow until it enters a lymphatic vessel which allows it to move into the circulatory system of the host's blood. Within a matter of weeks the *schistosome* worms are fully mature, paired in the bladder's veins, and ready to repeat this life cycle all over again.

(*b.* Courtesy of A. W. Cheever, National Institute of Health, Bethesda, Maryland.

e. Courtesy of D. J. McLaren, National Institute for Medical Research, London.

f. Courtesy of S. Carlisle, Department of Medicine, University of Pennsylvania.)

115

STRONGYLOIDES, AS OVA, LARVA AND ADULT
WORMS, IN THE TISSUE OF THE HUMAN BOWEL
(Magnification, 100X.)

Strongyloidiasis was another of the parasitc infections that afflicted the Nile dwellers of ancient
Egypt. The female worm lays eggs that hatch in the
intestine, so that the first larval stage is passed in
the feces. A more mature filariform larva develops
in damp soil, and subsequently penetrates the
human skin. Eventually the larva move from the
blood vessels into the lungs and there mature into
adolescent worms. Full maturity is achieved in the
small intestine, to set the life cycle of the parasite
in motion once more.

The recent autopsy of the mummified intestinal tissue of an adult female named Asru (of the Twenty-
fifth Dynasty: Manchester Museum: 1777) revealed
the remains of this infestation in significant detail.

(Courtesy of the Department of Parasitology, University of Pennsylvania)

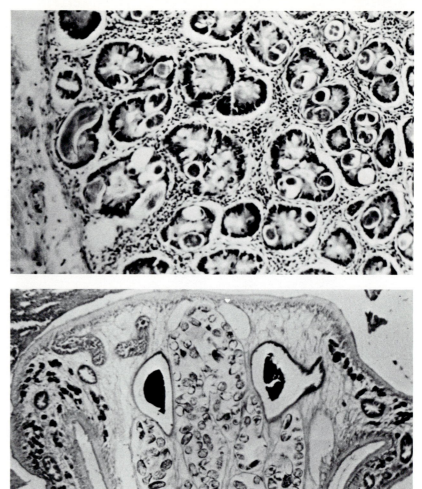

116

LIVER FLUKE (*FASCIOLA HEPATICA*) SHOWN
IN SITU, IN A MICROSECTION OF HUMAN LIVER
TISSUE
(Magnification, 40X.)

This parasite has a life cycle very similar to that of
schistosomiasis (see **113**) except that the *cercariae*
contaminate water plants (especially watercress)
eaten by man. Evidence for liver fluke as a disease
in ancient Egypt was recently obtained in an autopsy
of liver tissue embalmed with the two brothers,
Nakht-Ankh and Khnum-Nakht, in Manchester Museum (21470 and 21471).

(Courtesy of the Department of Parasitology, University of Pennsylvania)

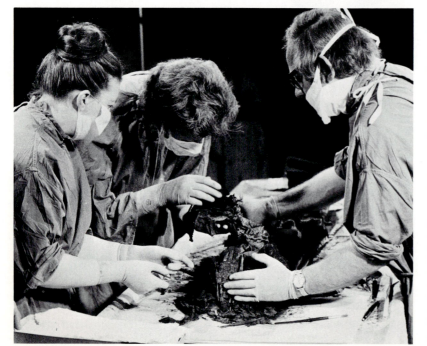

117

AUTOPSY IN PROGRESS AT THE MEDICAL
SCHOOL OF MANCHESTER UNIVERSITY,
IN JUNE, 1975

The mummy under scrutiny was an unidentified girl
aged about thirteen years. She seems to have lived
during the Twenty-first Dynasty, *circa* 1000 B.C., but
to have been re-wrapped for some reason during
the fourth century A.D.

The autopsy of this mummy proved particularly interesting because the calcified remains of a guinea
worm were detected in the right side of the abdomen. Guinea worm (*Dracunculus medinensis*), like
Schistosomiasis and *Strongyloides* (**114** and **115**), is
a parasite that bred freely in the Nile environment
in ancient times. The female worm discharges larvae through a blister in the skin that bursts on contact with fresh water. The infective larval stage is
hosted by a microorganism (called *Cyclops)* which
is swallowed by human beings as a contaminant of
drinking water. One of the major hazards of guinea
worm infection is the possibility of gangrene de-
veloping when bacteria invade the tissue within the
broken blister.

(Courtesy of Dr. A. R. David, Manchester Museum)

BIBLIOGRAPHY

Baines, J., and J. Málek
1980
Atlas of Ancient Egypt. Phaidon, Oxford

Binford, C. H., and D. H. Connor (editors)
1976
Pathology of Tropical and Extraordinary Diseases II . Armed Forces Institute of Pathology, Washington, D.C.

Breasted, J. H.
1909
A History of Egypt. Charles Scribner's Sons, New York

Brothwell, D., and A. T. Sandison (editors)
1967
Diseases in Antiquity. C. C. Thomas, Springfield, Illinois

Cockburn, A., R. A. Barraco, T. A. Reyman, and W. A. Peck
1975
"Autopsy of an Egyptian Mummy"; *Science,* 187, 1115-1160

Darby, W. J., P. Ghalioungui, and L. Grivetti
1977
Food: The Gift of Osiris I and II. Academic Press, New York

David, A. R. (editor)
1979
Manchester Museum Mummy Project, Manchester University Press, Manchester

Ebbell, B.
1937
The Papyrus Ebers. Levin and Munksgaard, Copenhagen

Harris, J. E., and K. R. Weeks
1973
X-raying the Pharaohs. Charles Scribner's Sons, New York

Ruffle, J.
1977
Heritage of the Pharaohs. Phaidon Press, Oxford

Winlock, H. E.
1941
Materials used at the Embalming of King Tutankh-amun. The Metropolitan Museum of Art, New York: Occasional Papers 10